IMAGES OF ENGLAND

Around
Uckfield

The old part of Uckfield at the top of the High Street has changed remarkably little in the past hundred years. That this is so is due to the efforts of several organisations and to a number of determined men and women, but to none more than Tony Turner, who died in August 1997. Tony lived for many years at 224, High Street (immediately behind the sign here saying 'Please Drive Slowly'). He was the founder, in 1968, of the Uckfield and District Preservation Society; he was instrumental in saving Nutley Windmill from collapse and Bridge Cottage from the developers' grasp; he had a deep knowledge of building history and construction methods and he was himself a consummate and meticulous craftsman. The members of the Society he founded dedicate this book to his memory.

IMAGES OF ENGLAND

Around
Uckfield

Uckfield and District Preservation Society

NONSUCH

The Uckfield and District Preservation Society was founded in 1968 to save a windmill from collapse. Since then the Society has not only brought Nutley Mill back to working order but has also carried out restoration work on Bridge Cottage, a fifteenth-century Wealden Hall house. The Society's local history branch researches the history of the neighbourhood and publishes the results in its journal, Hindsight. Equally importantly the Society helps the Town Council to guard against threats to Uckfield's historic buildings.

First published 1997
This new pocket edition 2006
Images unchanged from first edition

Nonsuch Publishing Limited
The Mill, Brimscombe Port,
Stroud, Gloucestershire, GL5 2QG
www.nonsuch-publishing.com

Nonsuch Publishing is an imprint of Tempus Publishing Group

British Library Cataloguing in Publication Data.
A catalogue record for this book is available from the British Library.

ISBN 1-84588-328-4

Typesetting and origination by Nonsuch Publishing Limited
Printed in Great Britain by Oaklands Book Services Limited

Contents

Acknowledgements

This book has been produced as the result of a concerted effort by the local history branch of the Uckfield and District Preservation Society (U.D.P.S.). Nevertheless it would be wrong not to acknowledge the contribution made by individuals, not all of them members of the Society. Norman Edwards and Michael Harker put their entire collections of postcards and photographs at our disposal. Peter Kirby allowed us to plunder his albums, which are particularly strong on the outlying villages. Roy and Barbara Fuller, Bert and June Mugridge, Mary Fox, Derek Thorpe, Peter Gillies, Michael Cyster, Debbie McDonnell, Bob Dubber, Simon Wright (who also acted as editor), Wilma Ledward, Peter Ferguson, Anita Hewson, Betty Turner, Beatrice Veness, Luther Batchelor, John Browning, Rodney Weston, John Dibley, Gordon Cornford, Joan Power, John Holmes and Brian Hart have all lent postcards, prints or photographs, the great majority of which have not appeared in a publication before. Norman Edwards has been a mine of information and he and many others have patiently answered endless questions, while Keith and Pat Eves, Sally Pearce and Brian Phillips have ferreted out obscure facts from unlikely sources besides saving the editor from too many avoidable errors. In addition John Sharp has skilfully enhanced a number of faded old photographs. We thank them all most warmly. The text that supports the illustrations is drawn substantially from census returns and trade directories. Oral testimony of local residents has been of great value as well as the research of members of U.D.P.S.

Introduction

Uckfield is an unremarkable town set in the Sussex Weald. A King once stayed overnight (some seven hundred years ago) but the nearest battle was fought ten miles away, no treaties were signed within its bounds and no figure of national importance was born, lived or died there. How then can we justify the appearance of a book about Uckfield's past? It is the very absence of famous events and people that enables us to concentrate on the lives of its inhabitants – in work and recreation, in home life and worship. As we look at the illustrations we must try to make a mental adjustment that will enable us to see the world of, say, 1870 through their eyes and to judge for ourselves their aspirations and achievements, their attitudes to life and their assumptions about social behaviour. Try, when you look at the often tiny figures in a photograph, to remember that each one was a real person (whether child or adult) and that one amongst them may have been your great-great-grandmother. Try, too, to go beyond the superficial feelings of nostalgia – a yearning for 'the good old days' – and see the world as our forebears saw it, not as 'picturesque' or 'appealing', but as features of everyday life, some cheerful, some sad, some monotonous, some exciting, and all of them subject to very different standards where wealth and poverty, health and hygiene, belief and behaviour were concerned.

To that end we have tried to include scenes that illustrate most aspects of everyday life, though of necessity nearly every photograph was taken out of doors. Our aims have been circumscribed by various factors: (1) The photographer had to consider what scenes would 'sell' when converted into postcards. What we would love to know more about was so mundane to them as not to justify taking a snapshot. (2) Movement was almost impossible to capture when each photograph required a lengthy exposure. (3) To compensate for lack of movement, figures, especially children, were artificially posed and consequently often look stiff and unnatural to our eyes.

We have attempted to show the development of the town from the beginning of the nineteenth century up to the outbreak of the Second World War. Clearly, there were almost no photographs taken before c. 1860 and so, for the earlier stages, we have relied on prints, maps or photographs of a later date. It is important to point out that we make no claim that any photograph in any section of the book necessarily purports to have been taken during the period it illustrates. It does however represent that particular scene as it would then have appeared and we have tried hard to avoid obvious anachronisms. That said, we have attempted to show the gradual changes that were taking place in roughly chronological order, though it often seemed sensible to group together photographs taken at different periods illustrating certain themes such as schools and railways. Equally, some of the farming and rural craft photographs could well have been taken at almost any time between, say, 1840 and 1940, so little did the skills and methods change.

It will be claimed, justifiably, that we have failed to do justice to the neighbouring villages, several of whose histories are as interesting, in their ways, as Uckfield's. To attempt to do such justice would have been to double the size of the book. Besides, two or three of those villages have their own histories already. What we have tried to do is to show that the neighbourhood (roughly a 5 mile radius) formed in many senses the arms and legs with Uckfield supplying the body. In other words the produce of the outlying farms and the products of the town's shops and workshops complemented each other and resulted in a community of 4-5,000 people that was largely self-supporting.

One further point may need emphasising. Postcards are dependent on photographic techniques (e.g. the only coloured ones before c. 1950 were hand-tinted) and also on Post Office economic policies. When one could send a postcard for ½d (and few telephones existed) people announced their imminent visit on a postcard the day before, or reassured their hostess of their safe return the day after. Occasionally a more informative social comment appeared and in a few instances we have quoted them. But it is noteworthy that over a period of some fifty years Uckfield supported the endeavours of nine or ten photographers who sold their work in the form of view postcards at various outlets in the town. To them the local historian of today is unreservedly grateful.

Our story begins at the very outset of the nineteenth century. The first census (in 1801) shows that the town had 811 inhabitants and was thus no more populous than some of the villages within a five mile radius. It was essentially a farming community and indeed its upper High Street was an interesting mixture of homes, workshops, farms and inns. The advantages it possessed over the neighbouring villages were that it lay at the intersection of two routes: north-south (London to the coast) and east-west (roughly, Rye to Winchester). In addition, a 'cut' from the River Ouse to Shortbridge enabled heavier loads to be brought within two miles of the town. At a time when road surfaces (even on toll roads) were often appalling, waterways offered an alternative.

As regards the 'ownership' of Uckfield, much of the town to the west of the High Street belonged to the Streatfeild family and most of the town to the east (and much of Buxted) to Lord Liverpool, with smaller patches belonging to substantial citizens like Richard Hart. Fortunately for us Richard Shuttleworth Streatfeild commissioned the well-known map maker, William Figg, to draw accurate maps of each part of his estate. These maps, beautifully drawn, were nevertheless working maps to which later alterations were added. The first of them (see opposite) shows how sparse was the building in the south-west section of the town (i.e. from Church Street to the river). In Chapter One we attempt to give a brief survey of early nineteenth-century Uckfield, a glimpse of some of the surrounding villages and an indication of how the whole neighbourhood was dominated by the two great estates.

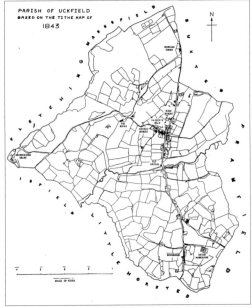

PARISH OF UCKFIELD
BASED ON THE TITHE MAP OF
1843

One

The Setting

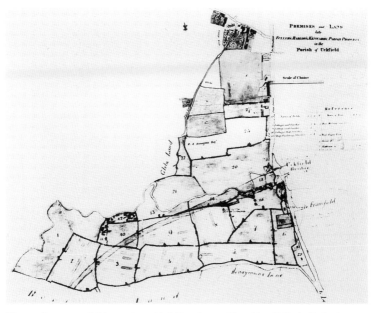

The northern part of this map is entitled 'Premises and Land late Fuller's, Barlow's, Kenward's, Parish Property,' drawn by William Figg. The southernmost part is entitled 'The Bridge Farm'. After it ceased to be a separate farm, the London, Brighton and South Coast Railway scythed through the middle of its fields. (Reproduced with the permission of the County Archivist, copyright reserved, ADA 229).

A coaching inn, variously known as the Red Lyon, the Maidenhead and the Maiden's Head existed on this site from at least the seventeenth century. In 1839 it was described as 'an excellent inn affording accommodation superior to what might be anticipated' and was used regularly as a magistrates' court and for important meetings such as those concerning the future of Ashdown Forest in 1830. In the nineteenth century, the principal licensees were Henry Cloake, Richard Cloake, Harriett Barnes and (from 1892) William Beaty.

Although Bridge Cottage lacks its original north (solar) wing it is in other respects a classic example of a Wealden hall house dating from 1436. Its occupants have been traced back to 1570 and for much of the eighteenth century were members of the Colgate family. Sadly, on Midsummers Day in 1799 the then owner, William Wood, and another man were carried away by a raging torrent and were drowned.

THE OLD CHURCH AT UCKFIELD.

The church at Uckfield, although of medieval origin, was never more than a chapel-of-ease for St Margaret's, Buxted, the living being held by a priest in charge. What it did, and does, possess was one of the earliest almost complete registers of baptisms, marriages and burials (dating from the 1530s) to have survived in any church in the country. Thomas Cromwell instituted the practice but in many parishes registers were not kept up or were lost or destroyed.

Nearly every parish had its own workhouse up to c. 1840. The building shown here was probably originally a farmhouse with two adjacent labourers' cottages. In the 1831 census it held no fewer than forty residents in the charge of a beadle. One of them was George Wren, a lad of 19 when he was charged with setting fire to a hayrick. As this occurred soon after the Swing Riots, courts were not inclined to be lenient. George was found guilty and taken to Horsham where, in January 1833, he was hanged.

The original Buxted village (Buxted meaning 'place of beech trees') was of Saxon origin but is not mentioned in the Domesday Book. It was grouped around St Margaret's Church which dates from the thirteenth century. The Hon. Charles Cope-Jenkinson inherited the estate when his wife died in 1814 and in 1828 he became Third Earl of Liverpool on the death of his half-brother, the then Prime Minister. He determined to move the village further away from his house and achieved his aim by refusing to repair the houses which gradually fell into decay. Most of the villagers had moved to new houses a mile away by the time of the Earl's death in 1851.

Ralph Hogge and Peter Baude, under the direction of William Levett, Rector of Buxted, are credited with producing the first iron gun cast in one piece in England (1543). Ralph succeeded to the office of the Queen's Gunstonemaker in 1559 and in 1581 he built Hogge House at Buxted, with the iron rebus of a hog over the north door. He died there in 1585.

Thomas Medley bought Buxted Park in 1711, pulled down the existing building and erected a handsome mansion on higher ground, typically early Georgian in style but with an added portico of double-depth Tuscan columns. It later passed by indirect inheritance to the Third Earl of Liverpool during whose time the young Princess Victoria was twice a visitor and returned as Queen bringing her husband and her mother.

In medieval times huge areas of woodland and forest were emparked, or, in other words, surrounded by a palisade with a ditch on the inner side to prevent the deer from escaping. From the eighteenth century onwards, however, with the growing fashion for landscaping, deer (usually roe or fallow) were maintained in parks as ornamental features and as a form of status symbol. Inevitably they were a target for poachers and as early as 1279 the owner lodged a complaint that 'certain evil-doers' had broken into the park and hunted deer therein.

In the Domesday Book, Ranulf held Little Horsted from the Count of Mortain. The church of St Michael is of Norman origin but was largely restored in 1863 by Sir George Gilbert Scott. Apart from a cluster of houses and cottages near the church, the village seems always to have consisted mainly of scattered farms, many of whose names can be traced back to the sixteenth and seventeenth centuries.

The heart of Newick is a wide village green with the main road cutting across it. The pump with a spout like a lion's head is dated 1837. From the green a street with cottages, inns and shops leads to St Mary's, an early medieval church restored by J. Oldrid Scott, and a mile further south stands Newick Park, the home of the Sclaters from c. 1700 to 1925.

Upton's Mill, near Framfield was built in around 1750, almost entirely of oak. It was owned for many years by the Newnham family but tragically on December 1, 1796, William Newnham's clothing was caught in the machinery and he was crushed to death. The last owner-occupier was George Heaver who worked the mill until his death, aged 96, in 1930. The mill was said to be 'never in want of water'. This view dates from c. 1910.

Framfield is another ancient village, called Framelle in the Domesday Book. The medieval church of St Thomas was burnt down in a fire of 1509 and subsequently rebuilt, but until 1892 it had no tower. This view, showing some of the old timber-framed houses, must date from after 1912 when the lych gate was erected.

The Manor of Maresfield was granted to Sir John Gage of Firle by Henry VIII. It owed its importance to the streams flowing down from Ashdown Forest which provided the power for watermills and for ironworks. St Bartholomew's Church, of Norman origin, was severely restored by J. Oldrid Scott in the 1870s.

From the Gages much of the property in the village passed to the Newnhams and in the early 1800s Wilhelmina Newnham, the sole heiress, married Sir John Shelley (5th Bart). Sir John later bought Marshalls Manor from Robert Holford who also owned Oldlands (see p.51). The Chequers, a fine Georgian building, has been an important coaching inn since at least 1734. This card was posted to Mrs Hewetson in British Columbia for 1d in 1915.

Nutley is a good example of a 'waste-edge' settlement, a village that owed its origin to families gradually encroaching on Ashdown Forest, cutting down trees and turning heath and woodland into arable and pasture. There had been an earlier watermill, but in *c.* 1836 Henry Setford erected a windmill, which he may have brought from some distance away, on a small field a mile from the village.

An Act of Parliament was passed in 1790 to make the Ouse navigable from Lewes to Balcombe. It was essentially an agricultural waterway with barges of up to 18 tons bringing chalk and coal upstream from Lewes and returning with farm produce. A cut, ⅝ mile in length, connected the river to Shortbridge where, close to the Horse and Barge Inn (whose landlord was also a coal merchant), there was a large basin. The opening of the railway in 1858 put an end to river-borne traffic.

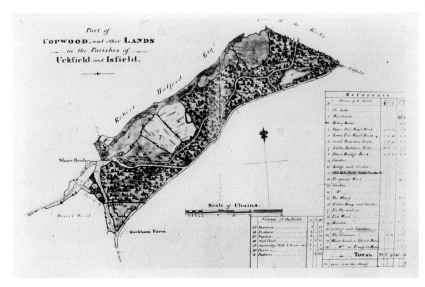

Part of
COPWOOD, and other **LANDS**
in the Parishes of
Uckfield and **Isfield**.

Scale of Chains.

Richard Thomas Streatfeild purchased the whole of the Rocks estate, which included Lake Wood, in 1784 and subsequently inherited the Copwood estate from his aunt. His son Richard Shuttleworth Streatfeild sought the advice of the well known landscape architect, William Gilpin, in damming up the stream to create a lake so as to make effective use of an outcrop of sandstone rock in the overall composition and also in the planting of a wide variety of trees. This is another of William Figg's maps of 1829 (reproduced with the permission of the County Archivist, copyright reserved, ADA 229).

Gideon Mantell, geologist, surgeon and Fellow of the Royal Society, paid a visit to Lake Wood on 10 August 1819. 'The scene was most enchanting; the lake was like a mirror reflecting the rocks and trees which overhung it', he reported. Unfortunately, when Gideon and his wife 'reached the borders of the lake a dandy looking young man who was fishing in a boat hailed us in an insolent manner and ordered us to quit the premises'.

Two

Early Victorian

The Tithe Commutation Act of 1836 affected almost everyone in rural England and Wales, either directly or indirectly (and has been of invaluable help to later historians). It changed the surrender of farm produce in kind to the incumbent (rector, vicar) to an annual payment based on current prices. In 1841 Richard Holman certified the sum to be paid by way of Rent Charge in lieu of tithes among lands in the parish of Uckfield at £315 5s (which included £30 for hops). This figure was based on a price per bushel of wheat at 7/- barley at 3/11d and oats at 2/9d. For every parish a tithe map was drawn, often the first reasonably accurate record of fields, roads and houses. For Uckfield the first five or six years of Queen Victoria's reign were a period of significant change with the building, or rebuilding, of the Union Workhouse, the Parish Church and The Rocks mansion, together with the setting up of East Sussex Police and of Penny Postage, in addition to the 1841 Census and the Tithe Map.

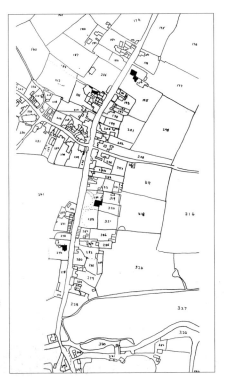

Left: In 1839 the whole of Uckfield old church, except for the base of the tower and a small part of the chancel wall, was pulled down and replaced by the present structure whose architect was William Moseley. The width of the nave was doubled by the addition of two side aisles. Mercifully, the early tombs and memorial tablets were preserved, the oldest (dating from 1610) being that of John Fuller, a member of the famous family of iron masters.

Below: The rebuilding of the church necessitated a reorganisation of the pews, a delicate matter since the position of one's pew indicated one's social status. Sadly, two feuding Uckfield families, the Kellys and the Wilsons, became embroiled in a distinctly un-Christian 'Pews War'. Until the rebuilding of 1883 the pulpit was on the right hand side of the nave.

The house known as The Rocks, built by Richard Thomas Streatfeild in around 1800, had a comparatively short life span. His son, Richard Shuttleworth Streatfeild, was only eight when he inherited the estate in 1813 but he was guided by the advice of his mother's second husband, Richard Prime. In 1838 he had the old house pulled down and a more imposing one, designed by Sydney Smirke, erected in its place. Here the Streatfeilds lived for almost a century.

Richard Shuttleworth Streatfeild died of tetanus as a result of an accidental discharge of his shotgun which grazed his foot with pellets. His son, Richard James Streatfeild, inherited the estate at the age of seven and once more Richard Prime came to the rescue to sort out legal problems. Young Richard thereafter devoted much of the rest of his life to the maintenance of this important estate and to his widespread interests in the locality and the county (see p.128).

Uckfield House was built in around 1827, probably for William and Mary Smith. In 1835 it was sold to Edmund and Sarah Kelly. Their occupation of the house was spasmodic since Edmund owned considerable estates in Ireland. After his death, Sarah (whose early life had elements of romance and squalor) remained at Uckfield, involving herself in disputes with the Maryon-Wilsons over the allocation of pews in the rebuilt Holy Cross Church. Much of the rest of her time was taken up in a prolonged legal battle with her late husband's relatives. By 1856 Sarah was back in Ireland where on 8 April she was shot dead by two men disguised as women who fired at her at point-blank range. The assassins were never brought to justice.

UCKFIELD HOUSE 44

Uckfield House	1	Edmund Kelly	75	Ind.	
		Sarah do	35	Ind	N
		James Herriot	35	Surgeon	N
		Mary Birch	25	Ind	N
		Robert Bayley	15	Ind	N
		Ellen Stewart	50	F. S.	N
		Patrick Sheehan	23	M. S.	
		Jane Gerraghty	30	F. S.	
		Ellen Moore	30	F. S.	

Although an unusually complete census of Uckfield for 1831 exists, it gives just the name of the head of each household, his or her occupation or status and the numbers of males and females in each. 1841 is the first year for which a reasonably complete census was drawn up for every parish in the land. On page 8, at Uckfield House, we find Edmund Kelly, aged 75, of independent means; Sarah Kelly 35; James Herriot, a surgeon; Mary Birch and Robert Bayley (Sarah's relatives), together with one male and three female servants (PRO HO 107/1116/4. © Crown copyright.)

Even before penny postage was introduced in 1840, Uckfield's Benjamin Piddington was a busy man since letters arrived (by coach) every morning at 3am and an hour later letters were dispatched to Hailsham and Eastbourne. Letters from Eastbourne arrived at 10.30pm and those destined for London left at 11.30pm. The cost was calculated by mileage and was normally paid by the recipient. This letter was written by Robert Moore of Fletching on 30 March 1822. It was addressed simply to Robert Rodgers Esq, Solicitor, Sheffield, Yorkshire, and cost him 11d (about £2.50 now).

> this is to inform you
> what you have to undergo
> Jentelmen if providing you
> Dont pull down your nes-
> shines and rise the poor
> mens wages the maried
> men give tow and six
> pence a day a day the
> singel tow shilings or we
> will burn down your
> barns and you in them
> this is the last notice
>
> from W B B

In the late autumn of 1830, as a result of a combination of poor harvests and low agricultural wages, a movement known as the Captain Swing Riots, originating in Kent, spread across Sussex and into Hampshire. In spite of lurid threats in letters such as these they were remarkably non-violent: no one was killed, no animals were maimed and few threshing machines were smashed. Even so, troops were stationed in the towns and villages around, including a single troop of the 5th Dragoons in Uckfield.

Transportation, from 1787 onwards, almost invariably meant to Australia or Tasmania for 7 or 14 years or for life and in any case few returned. For Uckfield and its neighbourhood we have figures only from 1812 and only for those sentenced at Quarter Sessions, not those sentenced at Assizes. In a period of forty years, 58 people (nearly all young labourers) were sentenced, mostly for larceny and the great majority for seven years. In the early days many were employed in gangs, building roads, harbours and other installations.

Above: The success of the Metropolitan Police, formed in 1829 by Sir Robert Peel, led to the passing ten years later of the County Police Act, giving each county the power to raise its own police force. In East Sussex, Capt. MacKay was appointed Chief Constable in 1840, his home, Hylands, at Framfield becoming effectively Police HQ. A police lock-up was built in 1841 in Hempstead Road by Stephen Markwick for £188. It had two cells and a common-room (for police business) on the ground floor and a bedroom and a living-room upstairs.

Right: Police Constables in the early days had to be under 40, over 5ft 7in, able to read and write well and to do simple figuring. They were required to record details of all their duties in a journal and of course their sole means of transport was on foot. Conference points were allotted to ensure that constables met their opposite numbers from adjoining beats on a regular basis. P.C. Dive, here shown in the earliest style of uniform, was stationed at Barcombe in the 1850s.

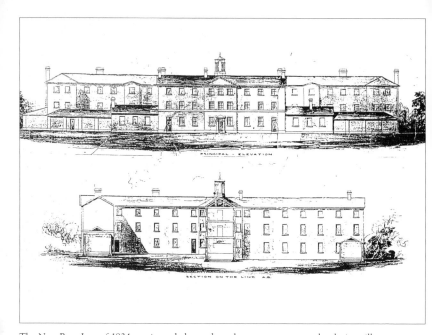

PRINCIPAL · ELEVATION

SECTION ON THE LINE A.B.

The New Poor Law of 1834 was intended to reduce the cost to ratepayers by closing village workhouses and concentrating their inmates in a single Union building serving a large number of parishes. By making the inmates work hard the authorities hoped to discourage those loath to find employment outside. The intention was also to provide separate accommodation for the aged and infirm, the mentally and physically handicapped and orphans, but lack of money usually defeated these hopes.

In 1839 the Uckfield Union Workhouse was opened to serve eleven parishes by accommodating up to 350 paupers. The architect was W.E. Kendall, a specialist in this field. In 1841 it in fact housed 152 inmates of whom 78 were children. It was run by a Master and his wife, the Matron, assisted by a schoolmaster, schoolmistress, men's nurse, women's nurse and a porter and was supervised by a Board of Guardians whose minute books make instructive reading.

Right: The foundations of education in Uckfield can be credited to Anthony Saunders who was Rector of Buxted for 46 years. In his will, in 1718, he left a schoolhouse in Uckfield and an endowment for the education of twelve poor boys, six from Buxted and six from Uckfield, in reading and writing the English tongue and learning the church catechism.

Below: The Rectory at Buxted, a house of Tudor origin, was largely rebuilt in 1694 by Anthony Saunders. William Clarke, best known for his study of Roman and Anglo-Saxon coinage, was Rector of Buxted for 44 years and was succeeded by his son, Edward. Edward's elder son, James served as a naval chaplain and also as librarian to the Prince of Wales. The younger son, Edward Daniel, achieved fame as traveller, author and early student of geology.

THE RECTORY, BUXTED.

Uckfield Grammar School came into existence as the result of Anthony Saunders' will. It underwent the vicissitudes to be expected of any school in a small town but in 1800 William Rose, who had opened a boys' boarding school at the parsonage in Little Horsted, moved his school to Uckfield and grafted it on to the charity school. Thereafter it took an increasing number of fee-paying pupils, both day and boarding.

The National School began in a building next to the Grammar School but in 1849 it was condemned as being in a dangerous condition. As a result, a sum of £1,175 was raised and in 1851 a new school was opened on land just south of Holy Cross Church with a separate infants' department and a home for the master and his family. Thomas Richards was appointed Master and served for twelve years before leaving to set up a private school off Framfield Road.

William Rollison became Master of the National Schools in 1863, a post he retained for 32 years. The log book he wrote up gives a detailed account of the lessons and attendance of his pupils, with many references to their health and reasons for absence and the annual reports of the inspectors, on which the school's finances largely depended. The three Rs dominated the timetable but Scripture lessons and learning the Catechism were also of great importance. The school's additional functions included acting as Public Library and Savings Bank.

The school grew steadily after education became compulsory and in 1884 the building was extended. Mr Rollison was assisted by his wife, who taught sewing to the girls, and by a succession of monitors, monitresses and pupil teachers, one of whom, Ellen Brown, remained all her teaching life at the school and is believed to be the young woman on the extreme right. This is the earliest surviving photograph of pupils, and dates to around 1905.

Farmers, on the whole, were not much in favour of schooling for children who were mostly to become agricultural labourers and domestic servants (and later wives and mothers). However, farm workers should not be thought of as ignorant peasants. Each man, from boyhood onwards, had to master a wide range of skills in order to cope with all the demands of farmwork. On his skill, his industry, and his health, depended - in most cases - the livelihood of a large family. When harvest time came round it was taken for granted that most able-bodied men would make themselves available. The men numbered in the photograph are: 1) H. Hemsley, gardener; 2) Albert Shipton, railway porter; 3) Napkin Brooker, wheelwright; 4) James Sawyers, gamekeeper; 5) James Salter, gardener; 6) Joshua Hollobon, blacksmith; 7) Owen Crowhurst, head keeper; 8) D. Johnson, gardener; 9) W. Reed, shoemaker; 10) Thomas Kenward, gas man; 11) Thomas Wood, butler; and 12) Thomas Jupp, schoolboy. Hemsley and Shipton are winnowing and Sawyers inspecting the result. Johnson is turning the handle of the threshing machine, while Crowhurst holds a beer bottle over his head. Reed is about to pour himself a drink. These are mostly young men, it's a lovely summer's day (in 1863) and photography is a distinct novelty. No wonder young Thomas Jupp, free from school, seems to be enjoying his day's work.

Opposite: Charcoal burning was the method by which fuel for the Sussex iron industry was obtained from earliest times and even after the industry left Sussex in the eighteenth century charcoal burners were to be found at work on Ashdown Forest and elsewhere in the Weald. Each timber stack had to be accurately constructed averaging 45ft in circumference and 6ft in height and containing some seven thousand logs, usually of oak, birch or chestnut, with a central vent and flues. Each stack burnt for three or four days during which time the timber was slowly converted into charcoal. John Tasker (right) and his son, Alfred, of Crowborough, continued to practise the ancient craft until the Second World War.

Oxen were used for ploughing the heavy soils of the Weald from earliest times up to the twentieth century. On Downland farms the treading of the soil by their cloven hooves did valuable work in making a 'season' resulting in better crops of all kinds. This team was photographed in 1903 outside the entrance to Possingworth Park, with Bob Stevenson the oxherd and Jack Evenden his assistant.

Above: One needs constantly to be reminded that the homes where farm labourers brought up large families were rural slums whose only superiority over urban slums lay in the fact that the children, of necessity, spent the greater part of the day out in the fresh air. Arrangements for cooking, for sanitation and for sleeping horrified those members of the gentry and the clergy brave enough to investigate. This is the Trug Maker's cottage in Maresfield (1894).

Left: Although dressed for the carnival in 1911 as one of a group of farm yokels from Hadlow Down, this man has purposely accoutred himself as a Victorian farm labourer would have done: straw hat, smock and trousers tied below the knees. He carries a scythe with the blade folded back across his shoulder, a flail in his right hand and a bill hook in a plaited bag. One box may have contained simple medicaments for sheep or cattle and the other his bread and cheese. He smokes a clay pipe.

Three

The Coming of
the Railway

An Act of Parliament was passed in 1857, authorising the construction of a railway line between Lewes and Uckfield with stations at Barcombe Mills and Isfield. To raise the money 1,100 shares were sold at £50 each. The line was opened on 18 October 1858 and the actual running of the railway was taken over by the London, Brighton and South Coast Railway (LB and SCR). Ten years later the line was extended to link up with the London-Hastings line at Tunbridge Wells. The photographs in this chapter show how the coming of the railway influenced the growth and economy of Uckfield, and how new money led to the building of imposing country houses employing large numbers of indoor and outdoor staff, and to a general expansion of trade.

The original locomotive, No.130, built by J.C. Craven proved inadequate when the line was extended. No.27 'Uckfield', built by Stroudley, is typical of the locomotives (class D, tank, 0-4-2) used on the line from around 1870 onwards. Each had the driver's name painted inside and some locomotives remained in service for 70 years, achieving a million miles on the track. At one stage the experiment was made of converting from coal to oil-burning but the sulphur content caused black smoke to be emitted and had an unfortunate laxative effect on the crew!

Since Uckfield was originally intended as a terminus, the station was built parallel to the road and hence at right angles to the railway line. When the line was extended it became necessary to alter the position of the station, a task achieved by dismantling the wooden structure and re-erecting it alongside the railway line. This photograph was taken between 1896 (when the footbridge was built) and 1901.

In 1894 a further improvement to the line was made by the doubling of the track between Uckfield and Eridge, permitting 'a vastly improved train service' with 13 trains a day in each direction. The train arriving at Platform 1 is drawn by Gladstone class locomotive 197, originally named Jonas Levy. The locomotive built in 1888 covered over 1,200,000 miles before being finally withdrawn from service in 1932.

The wooden station was replaced in 1901 by the structure seen here. The photograph, one of a large number taken in the early years of the twentieth century by Windsor Spice is of particular interest not only in showing the impressive new railway station and footbridge but also a representative sample of most of the forms of terrestial transport then available.

Henry George Peerless became Station Master in 1903, soon after the new station was built and he lived in the flat over the offices. Immediately to his right is Mr Wilkinson, head porter, and beyond him the rest of the station staff. The coming of the railway had a dramatic effect on every aspect of commercial life from farming of every kind, through rural industries, to shopkeeping. The products of the farms, corn, meat, milk, hops, chickens etc. could be transported far afield relatively cheaply and goods manufactured elsewhere in Britain and abroad could be purchased in the shops.

The growing of hops was introduced to England by Flemish merchants in the early fifteenth century. Added to ale, they make beer which is bitter in taste and keeps much longer. It was always a labour-intensive industry both in the preparation and in the harvesting. These photographs were taken at Park Field, Cooper's Green, in a hop field rented by Vallance Taylor (of Mockbeggars Farm) from Buxted Park Estate.

There were hop fields on most of the big farms around Uckfield throughout the nineteenth century and, in contrast to much of Kent where the hop-picking was carried out by families from the poorer parts of London (it was their annual 'holiday'), in Sussex most of the labour was local. Schools broke up for the 'hop-picking' holidays at the beginning of September and resumed, normally, in the second week in October.

Farms which grew hops nearly always possessed their own oast house. Hops when picked were taken to the oast in pokes (loosely woven sacks to prevent the hops from sweating). The hops were then dried on a kiln over a furnace using charcoal and anthracite before being carefully spread out on the upper floor of the oast and finally pressed tightly into pockets, long sacks weighing 1½ cwt when full. These pockets at Hempstead Farm are about to be transported to the brewery.

From the various farms the pockets of hops were taken by cart to one of the local breweries. The brewing process normally occupied up to six months before the beer was kegged and sent out to the public houses in Uckfield itself and the neighbouring villages. These pubs often acted also as collecting points for chickens which had been fattened on the farms (see p. 38). The waggon here is loaded with pedds (baskets), made of willow. The Barley Mow, two miles south of Uckfield, in spite of being relatively isolated, was usually well-patronised.

Wheat was an important crop in the Weald from Roman times but its importance declined with the coming of the railway. This photograph was taken on Great Birdneye Field on Harlands Farm, though the buildings in the background are actually those of Birdneye Farm, both farms then being part of the Buxted Park Estate.

From the twelfth until the eighteenth century, the open-trestle postmill was a familiar sight all over eastern and south-eastern England. The buck of the mill rotated round the centre post and the tailpole kept the sweeps pointed into the wind. Nutley Mill was erected by Henry Setford in around 1836. A later miller, William Taylor, seen here in 1890, renewed much of the machinery, but by then old-fashioned windmills were under severe economic pressure and Nutley ceased operating in 1908.

Right: The windmill at Cross-in-Hand is similar to the one at Nutley but here the trestle is enclosed in a roundhouse (which gives protection and storage space) and the fantail turns the mill into the wind automatically. The mill was originally at Mount Ephraim, Uckfield (close to the Barley Mow), but was moved in around 1850 to a site three miles further east. However, when Possingworth Manor (see also p.50) was being built the mill was found to overlook the house. Louis Huth therefore paid to have the mill removed and re-erected at Cross-in-Hand where it continued to operate, grinding animal feed, until 1969.

Below: Richard Pratt had this mill built at Crowborough in 1861 at a cost of £1,000. This was a tower mill with a solid base, the tower tile-hung and the sweeps attached to a cap whose direction was controlled by the fantail. Richard's elder son Jesse was killed when his smock became trapped in the mill machinery as he was dressing a millstone. Samuel, the younger son, took over in 1877 and operated the mill until his death in 1895. It finally stopped working in 1911.

Left: Uckfield probably had a water-mill from very early times, but in 1792 the existing structure was rebuilt as a five storey building by Caleb Pearce with an iron breastshot wheel 18ft in diameter and 4ft 6in wide, driving mainly iron machinery. A century later the mill was greatly enlarged by Edwin Kenward. He put up a five storey building alongside the railway, specifically designed to house large steel rollers powered by a 24in Little Giant water turbine, installed by James Dadswell of nearby Brunswick House.

Below: The Kenwards had played an important part in the development of Uckfield in the second half of the nineteenth century. Tragically, Edwin was found drowned in the river near the mill in April 1905. The mill was then taken over by Ebenezer Warburton who had married Harriet, daughter of George Heaver. In 1922 he replaced the middle section of the mill with a four-storeyed building and the mill continued to operate until 1950.

ROLLER MILLS, UCKFIELD, SUSSEX.

Hempstead Mill is a good example of a building which has adapted to a variety of purposes. The earliest reference (in 1756) describes it as a fulling mill. In 1795 it is marked on Gream's map as an oil mill and in 1806 it is described as a cotton mill. By 1838 it had reverted to flour milling, often worked in conjunction with Uptons Mill at Framfield (see p.18) and Uckfield Mill. The mill house appears to be older than the mill itself and seems to have been built in connection with a still earlier industry.

The earliest documented reference to Isfield Mill records that Edward Heaver could supply eight sacks of flour daily. This was in 1803 when the country was threatened by invasion. A century later the Isfield Milling and Baking Co. purchased the mill and installed a double horizontal 'British Empire' turbine, and enlarged the building itself. Dickson and Church took over in 1938 and operated the mill for a further 57 years, concentrating on pig and poultry meal.

Chicken fattening in Sussex is said to have started in Cade Street in around 1788, but it was not until after the railway opened up new markets that the trade became a rural industry. The chicks came mainly from neighbouring counties. On arrival at farms in the Heathfield-Uckfield area they were housed in pens with a feeding trough extending along the front of each row. After ten days the process of fattening began using the cramming machine. By means of a foot treadle a mixture of skimmed milk, animal fat and ground oats from the Argentine was force-fed into the crop of each bird through a tube. After three weeks the plump bird was killed and then compressed into the required shape. The result was termed a Surrey fowl. By 1893 over a million chickens were dispatched annually to London by train from Heathfield and Uckfield. In one record week in Jubilee year 47 tons 15 cwt were sent. Here a young soldier on leave operates the machine at Spoods Farm, Hadlow Down.

From at least the late eighteenth century, Uckfield had held a cattle fair on 14 May and 29 August. With the coming of the railway an added impetus was given to the marketing of corn and hops and a fortnightly market opened at the Maidens Head. In 1889 the Uckfield Stock Market (shown here) opened for the sale of cattle, poultry, eggs and other farm produce on alternate Wednesdays. The August Fair gradually died out but was replaced by a Christmas fat stock show.

In 1870 the auctioneers Redford and Green held the first of their monthly sales of dead and live farming stock and in 1899 the Uckfield Cattle and Auction Market was established. Charles J. Parris had set up in business as an estate agent and surveyor in 1893. He was largely responsible for the development of new housing in Crowborough; acted as surveyor to the S.E. Counties' Agricultural Show for 47 years; was regarded as an expert in the valuation of tenant right and farm stock; and, for many years, conducted the auction sales at Uckfield Cattle Market.

Brick and tile making around Uckfield dates back to the sixteenth century but the great days of this important industry began in 1858 when Benjamin Ware went into partnership with Henry Tyhurst. The success of the venture was largely due to the great demand for new housing, following the coming of the railway. By around 1885, Mr Ware had opened and developed an entirely new site at Teelings Common on what is now the south side of New Road, Ridgewood. Here he eventually employed over 50 workmen and, in partnership with his son, Amos, marketed their products far afield.

Benjamin Ware was born in 1819 in Framfield. After the move to Ridgewood he built The Four Poplars Inn on the Lewes Road; later renaming it the New Inn. Eventually he moved to a new house on the Eastbourne Road, complete with crested ridge tiles and a wyvern finial. He played an active part in public life as a member of the Urban District Council (see p.88) and of the Local Sanitary Authority almost up to the time of his death in 1910.

The success of Benjamin Ware's ventures led him to expand the range of his products in the 1890s. He embarked on the manufacture of the elaborate roofing tiles and finials so beloved of the Victorians as well as urns, garden ornaments and flower pots (of which 40,000 a week were turned out). The need for the erection of new kilns and workshops for terracotta products led to the development of another site further west along New Road. This was named The Sussex Pottery, Brick, Pipe and Tile Works.

The heyday of Benjamin Ware and Sons, some of whose products are shown here, lasted some sixty years. When the Second World War broke out Government regulations required nearly all brickworks to close since the fires from the clamps and kilns would have guided German aircraft. Even so, the firm continued to operate, on a reduced scale, till the final closure in 1970.

Thomas Bannister set up in business in New Town in the early 1860s. The main shop known as Albion Stores (shown here) housed the grocery, drapery and outfitting side, with the furniture and hardware store on the opposite side of the road in what had originally been a millwright's workshop. Mr Bannister's horses drew the undertaker's carriage and were also called on to haul the Volunteer Fire Brigade's pump.

Charles Cartwright's parents emigrated to America in 1887, so young Charles grew up in a covered waggon travelling around Dakota and Kansas. The family returned to England and Charles eventually set up in business in the High Street in 1898, trading as fishmonger, poulterer and dealer in game. Every morning he left Uckfield at 4am and pedalled a solid-tyred bicycle to Brighton. He returned with his purchases by train with the bicycle in the goods van. Later he bought a Darracq car. His phone number was Uckfield 3.

Manchester House was originally a farmhouse in the upper part of Uckfield High Street. It was sold in 1792 with 82 acres of land to the Manchester Cotton Company for £630. William Dendy traded from these premises from around 1890 and in the usual fashion developed a wide range of enterprises. Eventually he sold the grocery business to H.W. Wilde and moved his outfitters department to the shop at the corner of Church Street and High Street.

With few, if any, hygiene regulations to harass them, butchers were proud to display carcasses in the relatively unpolluted air of the High Street. John Colbourne had originally built up a grocery business but when his son Herbert took over in 1902 he concentrated on butchery. He also built up a national reputation as a breeder and trainer of alsatian dogs for display and police work. His elder son, Dennis, ran the steam laundry in Framfield Road.

Fuller's Bakery in Church Street was established in around 1910 and delivered bread by pony and trap to the surrounding villages. In the First World War, when both men and horses were in short supply, the womenfolk stepped into the breach, delivering bread in hand carts. Not till the 1920s was motorised transport available and affordable.

Edward Muddle drove the Mail Van between Uckfield and Cross-in-Hand (the next posting stage on the way to Hawkhurst) twice a day in each direction for at least 30 years. Up till the First World War the letter rate was still 1d and the postcard rate ½ d. The photograph was taken outside Mr Muddle's home at Lankhurst Oak (Blackboys).

Bourner and Co. supplied a vital need at a time when road transport lagged far behind railway traffic, operating a service transporting goods of every description from Uckfield to twenty-two villages round about. They would also supply pair-horse brakes for cricket teams and pleasure parties and they acted as agents for a variety of companies. Their office occupied the site of a house once used by Mr Adams, veterinary surgeon and dentist.

Seven years after the first car seen on English roads, Mr Charles Catt of Nutlin Farm, Nutley (with a family of ten to support) began operating the first local public transport service in this area: a bus pulled by two horses. Every day, from 1902 to 1916, it left Nutley at 8.45am, arriving at Uckfield Station between 9.45 and 10 o'clock and leaving Uckfield at 4.15pm to return to Nutley at 5.30. The fare was 10d single, 1/6d return. The bus itself was constructed by Thomas Beale, Mr Catt's father-in-law and upholstered by Betsy Beale.

Enthusiasm for the Gothic Revival, coupled with 'new money' from commerce and industry and other sources, led to the building of some notable houses around Uckfield. The original Horsted Place was occupied by the Law family for over 200 years but in 1849 the estate was sold to Francis Barchard who at once had the old house pulled down. The new house was built to the designs of Samuel Daukes by George Myers (a pupil of A.W. Pugin) and incorporated Gothic features such as the magnificent staircase which had featured in the Great Exhibition. It was constructed of red brick with black brick diapering and dressing of Bath stone. It remained the home of the Barchards until 1965.

The Huth family was of Hanoverian origin but had taken refuge at Corunna, from which its members were rescued and brought to England by the Royal Navy in 1809. Settled in London they became famous as merchant bankers. Louis Huth commissioned Matthew Digby Wyatt to design an imposing Gothic edifice, Possingworth Manor, near Waldron at a cost of £60,000. The builder was Alexander Cheale (see p.80). Because of the slope of the ground it has three storeys on the entrance (northern) side and four on the garden side (shown here).

On this site for at least three centuries stood a farmhouse called Puckstye. In 1865 a Victorian poet, Coventry Patmore, bought the farm together with an estate on the opposite side of the road. He commissioned a young architect, J.F. Bentley, to design a country house which he named Heron's Ghyll and he himself concentrated on the layout of the grounds with lakes and trees. It later became the property of the Duke of Norfolk and the home of his widowed mother, her three daughters and four orphaned grandchildren. Eventually the youngest grandchild, James Hope, acquired the estate and added many other woods and farms to it.

Oldlands was the other estate acquired by Coventry Patmore (see above) though the only building on it was a sixteenth-century ironmaster's house. Patmore presently sold the whole estate to Alexander Nesbitt, who commissioned the building of a large house by Matthew Digby Wyatt, (completed c. 1870) and who died in 1886. The later owners included Mr Bonaventura Misa, the head of a firm of sherry merchants, Sir Frederick Eckstein, a South African Gold Mine owner and his son Sir Bernard who was a generous benefactor to Fairwarp. This is a more recent photograph as the discreet TV aerial reveals.

MARESFIELD PARK.

THE SEAT OF PRINCE MÜNSTER

Maresfield Park, of seventeenth century origin, had been considerably extended in the eighteenth and again in the nineteenth century. About 1880 it was bought by Prince Münster, at one time German ambassador to Great Britain. The estate included a large area covered with scrub and gorse but the Prince refused to be convinced by George Varnum that it was indeed his own property until he consulted the deeds. The waste land was presently turned, with George's help, into a golf course and in 1904 Piltdown Golf Club came into being.

High Cross House, one mile south of Framfield, was built by F.P. Cockerell, c. 1860, for Robert Thornton who lived there till his death (aged 53) in 1891. He was succeeded by his son Major Robert Lawrence Thornton whose involvement in county affairs, as J.P. Alderman, Sheriff etc. was matched by his service to Uckfield itself on the Urban District Council, on the Board of Guardians and on numerous other bodies.

Four

Victorian Life

Most of us have our own conceptions of Victorian life. Some see it as a period of increasing prosperity, free from major wars, with religious observances playing an important part in life, a slowly growing social conscience with regard to those less fortunate and a period of family stability with all classes knowing their 'station in life'. Others are keen to emphasise the low wages and appalling housing conditions in which large working class families existed, the paucity of schooling and the supposedly hypocritical standards imposed by the 'haves' on the 'have nots'. All we can do in a few pages is to draw attention to improved services, pride in civic endeavour, the variety of religious worship and the almost total lack of humane provision for those too old to work. This is the Bannister family, typical of the rising middle class of Uckfield, their prosperity based on trade.

Chas Leeson Prince

1880.

Dr Charles Prince moved to Uckfield in around 1820 and set up in general practice at his home opposite the Maiden's Head. His eldest son, Charles Leeson Prince (b.1821) joined his father in the practice after qualifying at Guy's. From 1845 onwards he began to record meteorological details and astronomical observations he had made with his own telescope set up in the garden. He also became a founder member of the Sussex Archaeological Society. In 1872 he moved to Crowborough, set up a new observatory there and continued to work until close to his death in 1899.

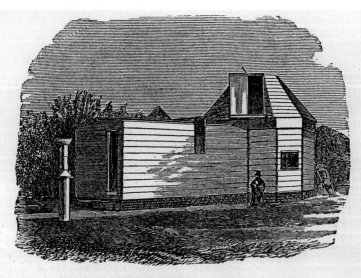

SOUTH SIDE OF UCKFIELD OBSERVATORY.

Above: Uckfield's first hospital built in 1881 was a gift to the town from R.J. Streatfeild. Known as the Cottage Hospital it was run by a committee, consisting of a Secretary, Treasurer, Lady Housekeeper and Medical Officer who gave their services free. The annual cost, including £4 (the wages of the sole nurse), was around £250 p.a. which was met by voluntary subscriptions, donations and patients' fees, the latter not to exceed 7/6d per week.

Right: Until near the end of the nineteenth century all Uckfield homes obtained their water from communal or private wells. In his report of 1881 on a serious outbreak of enteric fever (typhoid) Mr W.H. Power drew attention to the various forms of contamination that could seep into wells. The problem was overcome by the construction of deep artesian wells at Hempstead, the water being pumped up into a small reservoir near Uckfield House. In 1903 the prominent water tower was built adding gravitational force for the supply of water to the town.

A Gas Company was set up in Uckfield in 1859. In the next sixty years no less than five gas holders, each bigger than its predecessor, were constructed. The one shown here (put up in 1908) is the fourth in the series. By then gas, for lighting and heating, was available to almost anyone in the town who could afford it. Gasholders in themselves are not considered romantic structures but the original of this postcard was sent by Wallace Chisholm (Bandmaster) to Emily Pelling, who duly became Mrs Chisholm.

The question of main drainage was an exceptionally difficult one for small, and certainly not affluent, rural communities in the days before effective local government. Cost, effectiveness and even the need, were hotly debated. Nevertheless a start to the installation of a drainage system was made by the 1870s and added impetus was given by W.H. Power's report. Here a gang of workmen are laying a drain in Framfield Road (c. 1900).

In the late 1860s the Uckfield Volunteer Fire Brigade was established. It was based at the forge in New Town and, appropriately, Luther White the blacksmith was the first captain. He was succeeded in 1878 by Frederick French and he in turn by Luther Martin, shown here with the Brigade's hand-propelled hose cart and, behind, the horse-drawn manually operated pump. When the alarm went Tom Bannister of Albion Stores manhandled the appliance into the road while someone else went to fetch horses, which could usually be aquired from Mr Bourner. On one occasion, we are told, Tom lost control of the appliance which careered down the hill with Tom between the shafts, his beard flying in the wind.

Since there was no ambulance service in those days the 'corpse' must be assumed to be a first-aid training volunteer. By 1920 the manual pump had been replaced by a steam pump but the fire engine was still horse-drawn. Prior to 1905 it was not possible to summon the brigade by telephone.

Left: Until 1876 there was no minimum age for starting work. The majority of children were employed by their own parents, the boys in the field, the girls at home, and even when schooling became compulsory children were often kept away by parents who could not spare them. For boys, at least, the proudest moment of their lives was the time when they left school and obtained paid employment (even if only 2/6d a week) in the 'real world'. George Bingham Towner was a telegraph boy, employed by Mr Avis.

Below: There was no age for retirement, either. A man continued to work as long as he felt the urge or the need. In the case of farm labourers the need continued as long as his health (and especially his rheumatism) enabled him to continue the tasks he had worked at all his life. Fortunate (and rare) was the old man, if he were a widower, whose married children had room for him in their own tiny home.

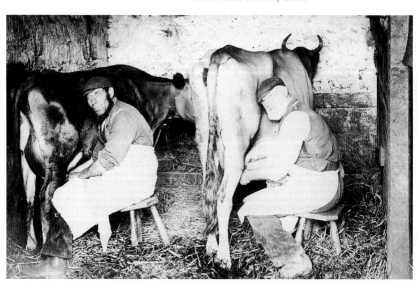

The great dread of all working people before the advent of Old Age Pensions in 1908 was that they would end their days in the workhouse. The particular severity of those institutions lay in the fact that men and women (and therefore husbands and wives) were segregated and could spend only a short time together each week. As time went on conditions undoubtedly ameliorated and in this photograph, taken in around 1900, an attempt to brighten up the men's ward for Christmas had clearly been made. In 1948 the building became known as High View House and continued to serve as an old people's home until its closure and demolition in 1977.

Although this is the funeral of a member of the Fire Brigade, c. 1906 (passing along Framfield Road) it exemplifies the hopes of most people then: that one's cortege and attendants should mark one out as having been a person of some substance, someone whose loss would matter to the community. Not perhaps an altogether unworthy hope.

Three things are needed for nurseries to become commercially successful: men with large houses who wish to show them off to the best advantage by surrounding them with parks and gardens; a reliable transport system to ensure safe delivery; and growers gifted with 'green fingers'. Around Uckfield the creative energies of men like Louis Huth, Coventry Patmore and Richard Shuttleworth Streatfeild fed the demand, while the railway companies supplied the means.

Uckfield was fortunate in having two enterprising nurserymen to supply customers' needs: James Cameron and George Piper (inset). Three miles further north, William Wood, as early as 1826, had started to turn an unpromising stretch of land, Tyes Gate at Maresfield, into one of Britain's most successful nurseries. His son, Charles, expanded the business until the nursery covered 100 acres, taking advantage of the railway network to send saplings, shrubs, roses and other plants all over Britain.

Right: At the time of the rebuilding of Holy Cross Church (see p.20) John Streatfeild, a distant cousin of Richard Shuttleworth Streatfeild, was priest-in-charge. A widower, he lived at Coombe Bank with his sister and two daughters. Not till 1846 was the parish finally separated from Buxted and even then Mr Streatfeild remained perpetual curate. He was succeeded, in 1863, by the Revd Edward Cardale who, two years later, was officially designated Rector.

Below: Coombe Bank, built 1820, was the property of the Streatfeild family. The estate, of some fifteen acres, included Hunters Pit from which sandstone for building purposes was quarried. After John Streatfeild's death it became the home of Major Bertie Shiffner, who also had family connections with the Streatfeilds at The Rocks. Edward Cardale, meanwhile, built, and lived at, Belmont, later known as Grants Hill House (and remembered for the last sighting of Lord Lucan in 1974).

COOMBE BANK, UCKFIELD. SX.

Uckfield Church.

Holy Cross Church (see p.20) was further enlarged during the forty-seven years (1880/1927) that Edward Sanderson was Rector. The chancel was extended eastwards by 16ft and the original medieval window re-set at the east end. Later, in 1892, an organ, built by Thomas Brooke (see p.77), was installed, pumped at first by water, then by hand and finally by electricity. The Rectory, a commodious building in Belmont Lane, was built for Mr Sanderson in 1883.

Although the first recorded peal of bells at Holy Cross was on 4 June 1827, the practice was undoubtedly older. The team shown here comprised, from left to right: A.J. Pierpoint (3), F.J. Charman (tenor), J.A. Hart (5), N. Reed (4), A. Corsham (treble) and W. Burrell (2). On 20 May 1907 they rang a true and complete Grandsires Doubles (5,040 changes). James Hart was Bellringer and captain for 45 years, from 1902. Alfred Pierpoint's Golden Wedding, on 26 November 1949, was marked by the ringing of a peal of Parkers Twelve Part Grandsire Triples.

As villages grew in size, some becoming towns, and new settlements sprang up, the big old parishes began to split up into smaller units. Little communities dotted around Ashdown Forest, often miles from any church or chapel, were at last being supplied with places of worship, such as St Johns, Crowborough, Holy Trinity, High Hurstwood and (as pictured here) Christ Church, Fairwarp (1881). A tower was added in 1937.

Differences between Anglicans and Nonconformists were seldom easily resolved. When proposals for a town cemetery in Snatts Road were first discussed in 1881 it was proposed that two chapels should be built, one consecrated for Anglicans and the other unconsecrated for Dissenters, but the latter protested against the injustice of having to contribute to the cost of both. After prolonged and heated controversy the decision was made to build two identical chapels. They were designed by George Fuller, an Eastbourne architect and erected for £1,100. The first interment took place on 19 January 1885.

Left: John Wesley's breakaway from the Church of England met with strong opposition from many of the Anglican communities. Not till 1829 was the first Methodist Chapel built in the Uckfield area, in New Road, Ridgewood. In 1894 a wooden school building was put up on a site in Framfield Road and three years later a brick built Mission Hall was added which was to become the present Methodist Church.

Below: In 1773 Thomas Dicker opened his own home at Five Ash Down for public worship and in 1784, on ground he had given next door, a chapel was built and registered under the Toleration Act. The first pastor, Mr Dixon, experienced problems over the matter of baptism and the congregation split over the issue. Thomas Dicker's grandson made improvements to the chapel in 1852 and soon afterwards the Sunday School room was added. Families walked to the chapel from a considerable distance and spent much of the day at the morning and afternoon services and at Sunday School.

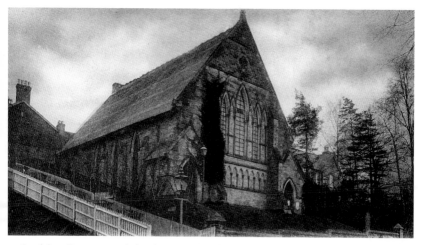

Land for a Congregational church was purchased south of the river from Alexander Cheale in 1862 at a cost of £105. Although Uckfield's entire population was then only 1,600, it was decided to put up a chapel which, with galleries, would accommodate 500 people. The contract (for £1,133) was awarded to Trayton Durrant and the building, in the Early English style, was completed in 1866. On 20 June (a Wednesday) of that year the Revd F.S. Attenborough conducted the opening service, preaching for about an hour on the theme 'The Strong and the Beautiful in the Christian Life'.

One day, in January, 1846, seventeen adults were baptised by immersion in the icy waters of Piltdown Pond and on another occasion a crowd, estimated to number a thousand, came to listen to a popular preacher. Since then severe winters have often provided entertainment for skaters and the summer months have attracted fishermen.

Thanks to the persecution of Protestants by Mary Tudor, to the Gunpowder Plot and to skilful Protestant propaganda, Roman Catholicism was regarded for centuries with a mixture of loathing and suspicion in England. Not till 1829 were RCs permitted to worship freely. At Heron's Ghyll a small RC community was fostered by the Dowager Duchess of Norfolk and it was her grandson, James Hope, who provided the money to build St John's Church which was completed in 1897. The church was consecrated on 7 September 1904 by Cardinal Amigo, who has Mr Hope on his left.

The first RC place of worship in Uckfield since the Reformation was a temporary iron chapel a short distance west of Ringles Cross Hotel. It was served by Father Ottley from Heron's Ghyll. When Father Fletcher (brother of Sir Henry Fletcher, MP for Lewes) arrived in 1885, the chapel was moved to a site on the north side of Church Street and a school, St Philips, was opened with Miss Fairclough in charge. In 1914 the iron chapel was replaced by the brick-built church, the taller building behind being the sick bay and laundry for the girls' orphanage run by the Sisters of Mercy.

Five

Uckfield at the Turn of the Century

The land which became Victoria Pleasure Ground was given to the town by Richard James Streatfeild in 1897 to mark Queen Victoria's Diamond Jubilee, but it had first to be fenced and laid out before it could be used. The opening ceremony was held on 28 June 1899 a month after the Queen's 80th birthday. The procession (halted for the photographer's benefit) was led by the band of Chailey Industrial School. Next comes a platoon of the 1st Cinque Ports Volunteers followed by members of the Urban District Council, Fire Brigade and the Town Band. The banner of the Tunbridge Wells Equitable Friendly Society, which had many members in Uckfield, is clearly visible. The official opening which took place on the Ground itself was marked by a short speech from Mr Streatfeild and a much longer one from Mr S.S. Avis, Vice-Chairman of the Council.

We have used this chapter to take you on a guided tour from south to north through Uckfield, finishing at Budletts, almost in Maresfield parish. Most of the photographs were taken between 1895 and 1905 and most were sent (at ½d) as postcards.

Until 1868 the road immediately south of the river was known simply as Uckfield Hill with only a scattering of small properties on each side. It started to be known as New Town when several of the smaller houses were removed to make way for substantial villas such as Albion Villa, Selborne Villa and Ulverstone House which appear on the 1874 Ordnance Survey map. The Railway Tavern, a Tamplin beerhouse, was built in around 1880, its proprietor, W. Hazelden, being also the engineer of the Volunteer Fire Brigade.

One of the most distinctive of the larger houses in New Town was The Belfry, built in 1892 by Barclay Watson, a lawyer, for his sister, Mrs Dodd, and occupied by the Dodd family for almost a hundred years. The builder was Alfred Chilton. Although this is a more recent photograph it is believed that the interior had remained virtually unchanged.

An attempt was made, in 1881, to provide education for boys at a more advanced level than that offered by the Grammar School. Calling itself The College and High School it was designed to prepare pupils for the Universities, the learned professions, the Army, the Navy and the Civil Service under the headship of Mr Frank Williamson. Sadly there appears to have been insufficient demand for the ambitious syllabus on offer and the College closed in 1894.

The buildings were purchased by East Sussex County Council and became the Agricultural and Horticultural College with Samuel Allison Woodhead as Principal (he was also Public Analyst for East Sussex). With lecture rooms, chemical and bacteriological laboratories and workshops and accommodation for fifty students it was well-equipped to provide both two-year courses (qualifying for a certificate) and twelve-week (winter) courses for farmers' sons. The acquisition of a farm (College Farm) at Little Horsted gave scope for the practical application of theory.

Henry Tyhurst who came from Aylesford in Kent was another fine example of Victorian energy and enterprise. Originally in partnership with Benjamin Ware at the Union Point brickworks, he remained in charge there when Ware opened his new yard at Ridgewood, but in due course moved his centre of operations to Framfield Road, developing a brickyard in the field on the south side of the road. These men are brickmakers at Union Point.

Henry Tyhurst built Aylesford Terrace, Mount Pleasant and, over a long period, most of the terraced houses along the north side of Framfield Road. He was in addition landlord of the Alma Arms, a coal merchant, insurance agent and estate agent. Among the large family and friends gathered round him are his son, Robert, and grandson, Guy, each of whom later ran the business.

At first it was only on the north side of Framfield Road that pairs or terraces of houses were built. At the east (right) end stands the Lion Brewery, originally owned by George Spencer Bourner and later by Francis Robert Bruce. The white building is the Alma Arms and between it and Abyssinia Cottages is a narrow alleyway now called Baker Street leading to an old mill whose roof top and sack hoist are just visible. To the west of Abyssinia Cottages stands Brunswick House, home of the millwright, James Dadswell.

In the early 1860s Croft Cottages were built by Alexander Cheale. One of the early residents (at No.2) was George Humphrey, the first stationmaster.

The Co-Operative Movement began in Rochdale in 1844 but the first Co-Op, a branch of the Lewes Co-Operative Industrial and Provident Society, to open locally was the one on the south side of Framfield Road which opened its doors on 21 March 1906. In those days every man as well as every woman wore a hat on almost every occasion.

Edward Dadswell, son of Thomas (see p.79) opened this bakery shop in Framfield Road in 1860, in newly-built premises leased from George Eade, the Church Street butcher. Edward's son, Thomas Edward, took over in around 1900 and at once had the new proprietor's name painted over the shop window and on the delivery carts.

In 1899 part of the Buxted Park estate lying south of Framfield Road was sold off for development. Harcourt Road, built in 1904, was named in honour of Lady Catherine Vernon Harcourt, an earlier owner of Buxted Park. On the right hand side the houses along the straight stretch were built by Edmund Bussey and the larger ones further up by Charles Pelham. At No.1 lived Bingham Towner (photographer), at No.25 Wallace Chisholm (bandmaster) and at No.30 (which is now demolished) Basil Johnson, insurance agent and evangelist.

To the Anglican Rector the threat of Nonconformity in the eastern reaches of Uckfield was a serious one. Who could be expected to walk all the way from Framfield Road to Holy Cross if the Congregational and Methodist chapels were so much nearer? The problem was solved by a gift of land, by the Hon. Henry Portman, on which a corrugated iron church (St Saviour's) was erected in 1904 with a small hall at the far end which could be hired out. The advantages were only marginally offset when it rained hard and 'you couldn't hear a thing inside the building.'

Bridge Cottage (see p.10) ceased to be a farmhouse when the farm passed into the ownership of the Streatfeild family in 1829. By 1841 it had become two labourers' cottages and the census of 1861 showed that it housed as many as eighteen people. As it was subject to inundation whenever the river flooded it cannot have been a comfortable house to live in. Even so, the last occupant, Mr A. Johnston, had lived there for sixty-nine years when he and his wife moved out in 1966.

The Uckfield Institute was opened to the public on 3 January 1887, its accommodation including a (non-alcoholic) refreshment room, kitchen, reading room (with games such as chess) and a large entertainment room with a platform for plays, concerts etc. At the back was a spacious bowling green. A coffee tavern, known as the Holly Bush, run by Charles Bellingham, was attached to the Institute.

This is believed to be the first appearance of a motor car in Uckfield, 11 April 1899 (Easter Monday). The car, thought to be a Benz, was taking part in a 1,000 mile trial in which the cars set out from London, journeying to a different S.E. coastal town each day.

High Street, Uckfield.

This parade of shops was gradually developed between 1880 and 1896. James Windsor Gould, tailor and outfitter, commissioned the handsome group complete with barge boards, Dutch gable and a terracotta frieze which housed Uckfield's first purpose-built Post Office (in which, in 1905, the town's first telephone exchanged opened). To its right was Bellingham's Temperance Hotel with the words 'Dining and Tea Rooms' over the shop front. The draper's and hosier's business (on the extreme right) was opened by David Wood in 1884. He handed over to George Newnham in around 1907 and in his retirement wrote a detailed description of the Uckfield of his youth.

Olive's Farm (probably of fifteenth-century origin) takes its name from a family who owned it in the eighteenth century. The farm complex, including barns (the largest of which appears to be of seventeenth-century construction) is clearly shown on a map of 1784. The expansion of retail premises in the nineteenth century led to the break-up of the farm and the gradual conversion of the farmhouse itself to shops.

Between the corner of Church Street and Bridge Farm there were few dwellings or shops of any kind before c. 1870. These stone-built cottages, known as White Rails, date back to around 1808. A family who lived at No.6 for many years were the Batchelors, William holding the post of Master of the National School and Clerk of the Parish and his son, John, becoming the famous missionary to the Ainu of Japan. The cottages were pulled down in 1894 and replaced by a terrace of brick-built houses.

The substantial parade of shops which spans the entrance to Grange Road was the work of Alfred Chilton, builder and furniture maker, working to the designs of the Brighton architect, Samuel Denman, the turrets being a distinctive feature. At the northern end was George Russell's The Golden Boot, next door The Library (Harcourt Smith) and at the southern end the printer, John Brooker, who published *Brooker's Guide to Uckfield*.

Under the turret to the north of Grange Road was Thomas Brooke's shop. He was a music dealer who sold pianofortes and lesser instruments. He also built an organ for Holy Cross Church and another for the Congregational Church and for this delicate work he had a 'clean air' room fitted up on the first floor. Behind lay a large property, Molesey Gore, the home of Frederick Brodie JP who (like Dr Prince) had his own private observatory in the grounds. Mr Chilton himself, whose own shop was under the southern turret, was a cabinet maker, upholsterer and 'complete house furnisher'.

The King's Head may well be the oldest hostelry in Uckfield and is certainly one of the oldest houses if one judges by the roof timbers. Captain Baker (whose title seems to have been an honorary one) lived for many years in a cottage nearby; he annually organised and supervised the torchlight procession through the town on November 5, the proceedings reaching a climax with blazing tar barrels being rolled down the High Street.

Below: The tall shop on the left, built in around 1860, was for many years an ironmonger's. The first occupant was Henry Faulkner who also ran a blacksmith's shop in Morgan's Yard. The next, John Etherton, took over in 1876, adding furniture dealing to ironmongery. By 1890 the business was being run by Walter Flint from Lewes. The smaller shop (out of the picture) next door was run as a draper's and outfitters by Clanmorris Thompson who also acted as Surveyor to the Urban District Council. The card itself (posted 16 September 1914) reads: 'Dear M, You ought to be here its lovely 2,000 soldiers staying here, they come up and speak to you. Jan and I got off last eve with T. mum's the word. Love Amy.'

For many years the magistrates' court was held in an upper room of the Maiden's Head but the close proximity of alcohol was felt to detract somewhat from the solemnity of the proceedings. In 1877, with money raised by a public company, land on the west side of High Street was purchased and the Public Hall was built. It was also used for meetings (on one occasion, in 1896, for a heated protest against compulsory vaccination), concerts and plays but its appearance was seriously marred in 1907 when the building was extended eastwards with a disappointingly ordinary frontage.

Mr T. Dadswell was the last baker to run a business at The Old Bakery on the corner of Church Street and High Street. His 'Banbury' pies were a speciality. Underneath the shop and some way along Church Street ran a large cellar, in popular legend 'The Bishop's Prison', but used more prosaically as a bakehouse. When the Old Bakery was demolished in 1891 it was replaced by a building with exceptionally tall chimneys run by W. Whiteside, and later by W. Botten.

Above: The importance of Church Street stemmed from its forming a stretch of one of the main East-West routes in Southern England (roughly Rye to Winchester). On the south side, beyond the Grammar School (see p.28) lay a row of cottages (known as The Strand) in the second of which lived the Pentecost family. Thomas Pentecost set up in business (*c.* 1825) as a leather cutter and in later years acted as Census enumerator and tax collector, but is best remembered for his poems which are homely in style but express a deep love of the Sussex countryside.

Church Street, Uckfield.

CHURCH STREET,

The ivy-clad house beyond Puddingcake Lane is Coppinghall. It was the home for much of the nineteenth century of members of the Markwick family. Thomas Shephard Markwick combined the duties and offices of auctioneer, valuer, census enumerator and inspector of nuisances and was a founder of the Uckfield Building Society. Many of his responsibilities were later assumed by his daughter, Agnes, who successfully filled the roles of Assistant Parish Overseer, Registrar of Births and Deaths and Collector of Poor Rates. Beyond, to the left, is the Malthouse, owned by Nelson Kenward.

Right: Puddingcake Lane is said to take its name from the simple fare offered to wayfarers and pilgrims using the east-west route through Uckfield. The lane led from Church Street past a few cottages, then down a steep track almost entirely enclosed by trees and finally across the fields to Coombe Bank. In two or three minutes' walk from the High Street one found oneself in open country.

Opposite below: The building behind the two small girls is Church House (though it was never the Rectory), a handsome Georgian five-bay house. It was the home for many years of Alexander Cheale, the builder of Possingworth Manor (see p.50), Croft Cottages and the Cedars. Its best known occupant however was the distinguished soldier, General George Calvert Clarke who led the Scots Greys in the (successful) Charge of the Heavy Brigade at the Battle of Balaclava (1854). In his retirement, and despite being confined to a wheelchair, he played an active part in Uckfield affairs.

Uniformity has its appeal but the charm of old Uckfield lies in its diversity and this is nowhere in better evidence than the upper part of the High Street, north of the East-West crossing. Here from Tudor times onwards grew up a medley of workshops, farms and private houses, the function of each often changing as ownership changed. The views on these two pages date from soon after the end of the nineteenth century when traffic was still horse-drawn (or leg-powered).

Bleak House, presided over by Samuel Stapleyhurst Avis, accommodated the Post Office (until 1892) and the Uckfield branch of Lewes Old Bank. Mr Avis also ran a stationery and fancy goods business on the premises. He was for many years Vice-Chairman of the Urban District Council and a noted public servant.

Probably the best, and most pleasantly varied, range of houses in Uckfield is the one on the left of our picture. Behind the brick, stucco and weather-board frontages stand hidden the timber frames of houses of sixteenth- and seventeenth-century origin. The saddler's shop run by Jasper Taylor and later by Mr Rice retained its Victorian atmosphere into the second half of the twentieth century. The double-fronted house in the foreground (Wisteria House) was a school for young ladies, run by the Misses Bowen.

Although the houses north of the Maiden's Head on the west side seem of less immediate interest than those opposite, each has distinctive features of its own. On the extreme right was a fishmonger's shop (John and James Griffin); next a sub-post office and sweet shop (Alfred Vinall); and beyond (in the white-fronted building) the premises of David Horscroft, leather cutter, currier, boot and shoe maker ('a noted house for homemade boots'); then E.H. Farr, pharmaceutical chemist, mineral water manufacturer and public analyst, and finally Manchester House (see p.47).

Mr Harden became the landlord of the Maiden's Head soon after the end of the nineteenth century. The old and the new sit happily together since the hotel continued to offer livery stables, while being listed by the Automobile Association. Later Mr Harden became landlord of the Alma Arms after marrying the widow of the previous landlord. He combined that office with Captaincy of the Volunteer Fire Brigade.

"The Chestnuts," Uckfield, Sussex.

This is an instance where the tree is more famous than the house, then called Red Tiles. Conkers have always had an irresistible appeal for small boys, one of whom would be stationed as look-out and on the shouted warning 'Here comes Mus' Cheale' the rest would scatter. Notice the deep gutters with steps to aid pedestrians, the gas lamp, the milk churn on its handcart and, in the distance, the tricycle with its rider receiving friendly assistance.

Richard Hollyman was an archetype of the Victorian entrepreneur. He started his business in 1849 and moved to Leicester House in 1860. He dealt in furniture and clothing, drapery and footwear, toys and games, besides acting as pawnbroker, valuer for probate and estate agent. His son, of the same name, took over the business in around 1899. Sadly, just as he was about to get married, he discovered that his bride-to-be was actually his sister. She appears to have accepted the lesser role of housekeeper with some equanimity.

Copthall appears to have been originally a single cottage later made into two. Copthall house was added on, at a slight angle, in 1875. At the same time the street lamp was moved from the roadside to a position where it illuminated the footpath leading to Rockhall Cottages.

The houses on the west side of London Road were built in the first three or four years of the twentieth century. Gas street lighting had been introduced some forty years earlier. The pony and trap was still the recognised mode of transport for short journeys by better-off people. The east side of the road was occupied by Cameron's Nurseries which extended from Brown's Lane to Henley House, the home of Mr Perigoe, the vet, for many years.

At Ringles Cross the London road and the road from Tunbridge Wells joined forces. The road had been turnpiked in 1752 and the tollgate was removed only in 1866 with the cottage being enlarged and turned into a grocer's shop. Disputes with drovers over the numbers of cattle and sheep must have been regular occurrences. Because of the drovers most roads had wide swathes of waste land on either side, on which thrifty men would begin by raising a cow or two, gradually increasing to a small herd, at no cost to himself.

One of the main drives across the Streatfield estates was the one constructed in the early part of the nineteenth century by Richard Thomas Streatfeild. It ran from Shortbridge Lodge in the west to Budletts Lodge, just south of Maresfield. The cottage on the right seems to have been a survival from that period.

Budletts Rocks were described by David Wood (see p.75) as a 'capital recreation ground for boys on Saturdays for hide and seek or hare and hounds'. They are one of the many outcrops of sandstone rock which occur between Uckfield and Tunbridge Wells. Weathering often produced fantastic shapes which appealed greatly to the Victorian sense of the 'picturesque'.

The story of local government in Uckfield begins as a result of the 1894 Local Government Act and in the photograph taken in Jubilee Year we are fortunate to see many of the men who made possible the rising prosperity of the town. Shopkeepers and traders, owners of mills and brickworks, a solicitor, a surveyor, a farmer and a postmaster (though a good many of them combined several roles) together with two notable landowners accepting leading roles in the spirit of 'noblesse oblige'.

A number of the same notables were present on the occasion when the drinking fountain and trough erected in memory of the Revd Edward Cardale was handed over; among them are Tom Bannister, William Dendy, Edwin Kenward and Clanmorris Thompson. To the right of the fountain appear the architect, C. Rapson, the Rector, Revd Edward Sanderson, and Gen. George Calvert Clarke (in the wheelchair). The whole scene, one feels, represents the apotheosis of Victorian England in the setting of a small town.

Six

The Edwardian Era

The era between the Diamond Jubilee and the outbreak of the First World War saw a gradual alleviation of some of the harshness of life for the poorer classes and an extension of the range of leisure pursuits for nearly everyone. It is marked by the advent of the motor car, old age pensions, secondary education, the cinema, boy scouts, the wireless and the aeroplane. Not everyone in Uckfield, of course, was to benefit from these novelties at least until much later. But sporting facilities were becoming more generally available and it seems appropriate to choose an introductory photograph that combines increased prosperity, leisure and a sense of security. It was taken on the bowling green behind the Institute (see p.74) with Bridge Cottage in the background.

This splendid vehicle is a Thorneycroft which originally belonged to Mr Baxendale of Framfield Place and was sold by him to Jack Thorne, the Uckfield Fruiterer and Greengrocer, who used it to travel to the Brighton vegetable market. On this occasion, however, it is believed to be taking members of the cycling club on an outing. The driver is Mr Thorne, the passenger Mr Paine, with Harry Hammond between them. The tyres are of the solid cushion type.

Balloon Descent at Maresfold 17.9.11

Left: Although the French were the pioneers of ballooning the first ascent in England (in 1784) was made by a Scot, James Tytler. Progress was slow and 120 years later ballooning was still a novelty with no obvious practical potential. This ascent (the postcard is wrongly captioned) was made in Maresfield Park, 17 September 1911.

Opposite above: The Coronation festivities (see p.96) had scarcely ended when Uckfield experienced still greater drama: the first recorded landing of an aeroplane in the parish on 2 July 1911 (a Sunday). The first aircraft, a Bristol Boxkite biplane (No.43), piloted by Eric Gordon England (a leading aviator living at Haywards Heath), landed safely in a field just north of the Victoria Pleasure Ground. In the days before fuel gauges he had come down in order to check his supply of petrol.

Two more aviators, Collyns Pizey and H.R. Fleming, were following Gordon England in another Bristol biplane (No.26) and they also landed in case Gordon was in difficulty. 'Unfortunately', as the local paper put it, 'on landing they collided with a small hayrick near Mr Siggs' house at Ridgewood' and their plane suffered damage. However, with the assistance of Aaron Horscroft (a carpenter) and William Brown and William Lockyear (tailors) the damage was swiftly repaired. When the two machines finally took off at 5.30am on the Monday, 'hundreds of people were up in time to see the start'.

A meet of the Southdown Hunt takes place in the station forecourt around the end of the nineteenth and the beginning of the twentieth centuries. On the right is the Bridge Hotel which had become the town's leading hostelry. In the background is the office of Bourner's, the carrier and coal merchant and in the far distance one can make out Edwin Kenward's roller mills.

Many village sports and customs are relics or survivals of pre-Christian times and the original maypole, often the trunk of a birch tree, was perhaps a phallic symbol decorated with garlands of May and spring flowers to represent fertility. Late in the nineteenth century a teacher at Whitelands College introduced the custom of plaiting the ribbons, by performing dances. This more decorous ritual chimed in well with Victorian morality and fondness for idealising country pursuits.

Right: All the big estates reared large numbers of pheasants and to a certain extent the prestige of a great estate depended on the success of the shooting season which began on 1 October and to which a great many guests were invited. Organising the large numbers of beaters and loaders was the task of the head gamekeeper, for this was the climax of his year's work, rearing the young birds, guarding them against predators and poachers and having them in fine condition for the annual battue. Samuel Kirby came to Maresfield Park in 1887 to be head gamekeeper first to Sir John Shelley and later to Count Münster. He died in 1916. This group is on the left-hand side of the photograph below.

Below: A rough shoot was normally organised by a farmer whose crops were the victims of rabbits, pigeons or squirrels. Anyone who possessed a shotgun would be invited along and asked to bring his dog with him. Hares were more plentiful then, too, and no doubt quite a number of foxes were bagged as well. Mr Hollyman (see p.85) is the bearded man wearing a smock.

The licensee of The Alma Arms by 1899 was Mrs Ellen White, widow of William. The pub acted as headquarters of the Uckfield Cycling Club, whose members are about to set off on a Sunday spin. Were the hats worn just for the photograph? The club disbanded when war came but was revived in the early '30s as the Uckfield and District Cycling Club by Sid ('Boss') Eves.

On Whit Monday (31 May) 1914 eight competitors assembled outside the Bridge Hotel and walked to East Hoathly and back, a total of ten miles. A challenge cup was presented to the winner, Whiteman of Battle (time, 1hr 34 min). Perhaps the motor cyclist and his side-car passenger exercised close supervision over the legality of the leading walkers.

The advantages of tug-o-war as a village competition were that it occupied very little space and cost almost nothing (once the rope had been paid for). If the publican provided the space he was more or less sure of thirsty customers. Furthermore as a man went on in life and his girth increased so did his value to the team. Fairwarp may have been stoolball champions and Uckfield hard to beat on the football field, but Maresfield could (and did) pull all the others off their feet. Mr Brown (with straw boater) was the electrician on the Maresfield Park Estate.

Uckfield had at least two football clubs in the early years of the twentieth century. This team, Uckfield Wednesday FC, known as Belmont Rovers, appears to have been based at the Uckfield Institute. Standing on the left (in overcoat) is FC (Ticker) Green. This was the last season before war broke out.

The 'Edwardian' period continued up to the outbreak of war, and included the Coronation of George V in 1911. In Uckfield the festivities spanned two days: Thursday and Friday June 22 and 23. The programme began with Church services at 10.30am followed by public dinners served on the Victoria Pleasure Ground at 12.00 and at 1.00. Then came sports, teas at 4.00 and 5.00, dancing and promenade concerts and finally a bonfire at 10pm.

On the Friday (June 23rd) the first event was a procession from the Public Hall to the Victoria Pleasure Ground where a Komic Kricket Match took place. The main carnival procession started from the Railway Station at 3pm when prizes were awarded for the finest costumes and the best decorated floats.

At 5pm after the procession had toured the town all the floats congregated opposite the grandstand outside the Public Hall where a 'battle' of flowers and confetti took place. Dancing, in fancy dress, went on at the Victoria Pleasure Ground from 7 till 10, rounding off two days of merry-making in unbroken fine weather. The arrangements were made by a special committee with Mr G.E. Hart as honorary secretary.

They were less fortunate with the weather on the following Sunday, 25 June, when a drumhead service was held, also on the Victoria Pleasure Ground. In spite of the pouring rain a very considerable crowd gathered and the solemnity of the occasion brought home to people living in a small rural community the awesome responsibilities taken on by the new monarch, titular ruler of some 500 million people.

The Revd Philip Fletcher was Priest-in-charge of the Roman Catholic Church of St Philip Neri from 1885 to 1893. He is credited with the formation of Uckfield's first town band, always referred to as Father Fletcher's Band. He stands, bowler-hatted, in the centre of the back row with James Haestier, Bandmaster, on his right.

By 1914 the Uckfield Town Band, under Wallace Chisholm, had achieved considerable local fame and was engaged to play at a wide variety of events. Here they are ready to perform at the Ringles Cross Sweet Pea Show in 1912. Left to right (standing): E. Avis, -?-, M. Grant, -?-, A. Picknell, A. Olive, W. Burgess, C. Parsons, E. Blackford, P.H. Shoosmith, G. Dumsday. Seated: E. Olive, L. Blackford, H. French, W. Chisholm, T. Dumsday, P. Route, H. Coussens.

A scene that captures the enduring appeal of farming to 'townies': haymaking in Luxford Field on a sunny day in June, with the hay being stacked just behind the Public Hall. The field was then part of the Grammar School's playing fields. Probably the four or five young lads in waistcoats had been given time off lessons to help. Operations are being supervised by the man in the bowler hat, William Holmes, of Birdnye Farm.

However picturesque to 'townies', farming in all its aspects has always been very hard work, often grindingly hard, and the occasions when a waggon-load of produce or material had to be fetched or delivered must have seemed like a half-holiday. The Cornford family farmed Harlands (previously Harlings) Farm for thirty-two years. Here Horace Cornford (bearded), his brother Eli and their carter (note the long whip) have been all the way to Mayfield to fetch a load of hop poles (c. 1916).

Above: The majority of people who did not work on the land or in shops were 'in service' as cooks, domestic servants, grooms, butlers, gardeners, etc. Almost every well-to-do household employed at least one or two servants. It is easy to condemn the 'Upstairs, Downstairs' structure but it was an essential ingredient of society. Here the butler, Mr Batten (right) and the head groom, Mr Thompson, enjoy a game of cards with other male members of the staff at The Rocks, *c.* 1911.

Left: Domestic staff in the big houses were miserably paid (for long hours) by almost any standards: kitchen maids and housemaids (£18 p.a.); cook (£50 p.a.); groom (£20 p.a.); butler (£70 p.a.) but for a young girl who had just left home (aged perhaps 12) there were the triple benefits of lodging and security, of a thorough training in most domestic skills, and the chance of meeting a sturdy young gardener with whom she might 'walk out' on an occasional off-duty Sunday. The Streatfeilds at The Rocks had the reputation of being considerate employers.

Above: The use of boys to climb up chimneys in order to dislodge soot had been forbidden by Act of Parliament in 1864 though no doubt the practice continued in places. Its need was reduced anyway when the labyrinthine chimney complexes of big old manor houses gave way to the more easily swept chimneys of Victorian builders. Many older people today will remember the elaborate precautions taken, covering all the furniture with sheets, when a visit from the sweep was planned. This picture shows William Ralph, eldest son of George Ralph who had a chimney sweeping business in Framfield Road.

Right: Before the First World War letter boxes were few and far between, so rural postmen collected letters as well as delivering them. Henry Towner's route, on foot, was from Uckfield via Little Horsted to Isfield and back. The local MFH had given him a hunting horn with which he could warn outlying farms of his approach. In his 41 years' service he walked 205,000 miles, for a wage of 12/- a week. He was the father of George Bingham Towner (see p.58).

101

The Headquarters of the Uckfield Police was moved to Lewes in 1846 but it was not until 1858 that Uckfield acquired a proper police station of its own, a building (later known as Thornbury) next to Arnold Cottage (see p.25). The growth of the town made the new station too small and a new site, opposite the west end of Framfield Road, was purchased in 1901. Work is seen in progress here and the new station came into action in 1905.

Uckfield Division (1905). Standing, left to right, are: PCs Anscombe, Bishop, Gibbs, Heasman, Edwards, Thomas, Keep, Teague, Shepheard, Sgt. Mead (centre), Crouch, Lancaster, Taylor, Lusted, Tester, Clarke, Rawson, Dilley, Heasman. Seated are: PCs McLean, King, Sgt. Kenward, Supt. Criddle, Sgt. Vernon, PCs Furminger, Hurd and Alce. James Criddle was the Police Superintendent from 1898 to 1917. In 1895 bicycles were authorised with the stipulation that no constable weighing more than 13 stone was to be allowed to ride one. Superintendent Criddle bought a motor-cycle and sidecar and received permission to use it to visit his out-stations.

The old stone bridge (see p.10) stood until 1859, when it was replaced by a cast-iron one due to the building of the railway. However, on 27 June, 1903, at 1.20pm just as a traction engine (weighing 9 tons and drawing two trucks) was passing over it, it collapsed so suddenly and completely that the engine fell straight down into the river bed. Mercifully, neither Horace Wright, the driver, nor Fred Bennett who was steering, nor Alf Yeomans, was seriously hurt, though Mr Wright was subsequently found to have cracked a rib. Dr Sweet was summoned and attended to the men's injuries.

The destruction of the bridge brought traffic to a standstill besides severing the town's gas and water mains, causing an escape of both elements. But so speedily did the respective officials carry out their duties that supplies were reconnected by 9pm. Mr Clanmorris Thompson, surveyor, meanwhile oversaw the repair of the sewage pipes. A powerful steam crane was brought up which succeeded in bodily lifting the traction engine out of the river. Work on the reconstruction of the bridge (seen here) inevitably took rather longer.

This was posted in Framfield as a birthday card to Miss Ruth Merchant at Horsted Keynes in 1906. It was taken, one would guess, in late September when the hop-picking holidays (usually five to six weeks) were drawing to a close. The boys look cheerful enough, some of the girls a little wary of the camera.

Blackboys National School had been in existence for eighteen years when this photograph of Standard IV (which mostly comprised ten year olds) was taken in 1902. If the photographer came only once a year it would have seemed a fairly solemn occasion. On the left is the headmaster, Samuel Williams, who was at the school for twenty-two years (1887/1909). His two daughters also taught in the school.

'Harvest home' marked the bringing in of the last load of corn and was a purely secular event, often of a bucolic nature. But on Sunday, 1 October 1843 the Revd R.S. Hawker, Vicar of Morwenstow, celebrated the first Harvest Festival at St Morwenna's. It soon became a recognised part of the church's year, but whether enormous chunks of currant bread were a speciality only of St Margaret's, Isfield, seems uncertain.

This photograph is undated. It was taken at Mount Ephraim near the Barley Mow, just off the main road to Eastbourne and may well depict five brothers and sisters. The girls wear pinafores and straw hats, the boys Eton collars and knickerbockers, indicating a well-to-do family. Guard as one may against false sentimentality it is not easy to dismiss from one's mind the onset of the First World War and wonder how many boys on these pages survived.

"SEARCHING FOR THE PILTDOWN MAN"

Enormous interest was aroused world-wide in 1912 by the discovery in a gravel bed close to Barkham Manor at Piltdown of what appeared to be firstly three separate fragments of the cranium, then part of the lower jaw and finally a tooth of a very early species of mankind. It came to be referred to as Piltdown Man. The discovery was made by an Uckfield solicitor, Charles Dawson, who had already made a considerable reputation as an amateur geologist and antiquarian.

The search, continued by Mr Dawson and Dr Arthur Smith-Woodward usually assisted by a workman, Venus Hargreaves, up to the outbreak of war in 1914, yielded no further important clues. The goose, Chipper, is said to have taken a keen interest in the proceedings. Mr Dawson died in 1916 and although Dr Smith Woodward later resumed the search, interest in Piltdown Man faded. It revived dramatically in 1954 with the publication of a book showing that Piltdown Man was a forgery or a hoax. Recent research has pinned the blame on Dawson alone.

Seven

War and the Inter-War Years

To the majority of British people the prospect of war seemed remote in the early years of the twentieth century. Since 1858 the only wars fought by the British Army had been in distant parts of the Empire and the only one of those seriously to impinge on the national consciousness was the Boer War. The Royal Navy secured not only Britain but the entire Empire against attack. The British Army, though very small, was highly trained and had been supported since 1907 by the Territorial Army (who trained in the Drill Hall). Here Royal Artillery batteries are at practice (possibly in Maresfield Park), the limbers drawn up close to the guns.

Like most other communities after 1918 Uckfield contrived not to forget the horrors and the tragedies but at least to overlay them with the joys of peace, weddings, babies, children growing up and the simple pleasures available to people in a small town. Uckfield had always had a reputation for making its own amusements in which young and old were equally pleased to join. At the same time farming and other rural industries carried on in ways that were changing very slowly. The chapter concludes in 1938, just before the inevitability of another world war became apparent to the people of the town and its surrounding villages.

Left: The prospects for a young man setting out in life in the early years of the twentieth century must have seemed promising. The British Empire extended across half the globe. A well-built young man might seek his fortune in Australia or New Zealand, in Canada or in the United States. Or he might choose to serve his country on land or at sea, or he might be tempted to lead a wandering life.

Below: He might, equally well, decide to stay at home, learn a trade, marry the boss's daughter, bring up a family and hope, one day, to run his own business as men like Thomas Bannister, Benjamin Ware or Edwin Kenward had done. And even if he did none of these things life in a small country town had its attractions and provided he kept his health and found a nice girl the future looked set fair.

Ernest Hoad, born in Uckfield around 1890, must have been typical of a whole generation, learning the baking trade (see p.72), courting and marrying Minnie Bedwell, bringing up children, joining in the simple pleasures and pastimes Uckfield had to offer and enjoying the companionship of young men like himself.

Then, without warning, War. We don't know whether Ernie volunteered at the outset or was conscripted later and details of his wartime service have not been recovered. But here he is, a stern and purposeful lance-corporal, aged about 25, and already well-acquainted with the horrors of war. But Ernie survived, as scores of his comrades did not. He returned to Sussex, sobered and saddened by what he had seen. Like millions of others his carefree young manhood had been snatched away from him and he faced an uncertain future. Like millions of others, too, the thought uppermost in his mind was: there must never again be another such war.

Above: During the First World War troops were stationed in and around Uckfield, ready to move down to Newhaven en route for the trenches. Many of them were billeted in private houses. Here a platoon is drawn up in the station yard awaiting transit. Would their average age have been more than 19 years?

Left: Many of the men, recruited from farm and forestry work, would have had experience of working with horses. Here an R.A. farrier is shoeing a horse at the New Town smithy. It is often forgotten what an enormous reliance was placed on horses by the armies of all the combatants throughout the war.

Opposite above: Arrangements for feeding constantly changing numbers of men, some stationed locally, many in transit, placed heavy demands on the army's logistics. At one stage the A.S.C. (actually Army Service Corps, but affectionately known as Ally Sloper's Cavalry) set up a cookhouse in the field behind The Holly Bush.

Funeral processions were an increasingly common sight in every town and village in the land as the mounting casualties on the Western Front, at Gallipoli, in the Atlantic and indeed worldwide brought grief to more and more families. In this instance the dead man was a Canadian soldier, stationed at Maresfield Park Camp, who was the victim of a traffic accident at Nutley. The cortege, a gun carriage drawn by three pairs of mules, has just passed the Drill Hall where so many local men had received their initial military training.

There are 93 names of the fallen recorded in Holy Cross Church. A memorial to them was erected in the churchyard and on 19 July 1919, three weeks after the signing of the Versailles Treaty, Peace Day was celebrated in Uckfield. There was a procession down the High Street, led by the Town Band, a Thanksgiving Service in the field behind the Drill Hall, a programme of sports for children in the afternoon and, in the evening and in spite of heavy drizzle, a series of traditional entertainments culminating in a torchlight procession and the burning (in effigy) of the Kaiser.

The War Memorial at Maresfield was dedicated in 1920. The scene here, though repeated in thousands of villages throughout Britain, has been captured with great sensitivity by the cameraman: the restrained grief of mothers and widows is deeply affecting.

William John Weston (on the extreme right) carried on business as 'Wheelwright, Coach and Carriage Builder' at the eastern end of Framfield Road for many years. He and Jane had seven sons and four daughters and on 8 September 1920 the youngest daughter, Edith, was married to Lancelot Vinall at Uckfield Baptist Chapel. Mr Weston died a year later.

While the horrors of war would never be forgotten, this happy scene, at Hooke Hall, Uckfield, in 1923 celebrates the regeneration of life after the years of slaughter. Mothers' Union, whose membership was open to women of all Christian denominations, originated in meetings held at Old Alresford in Hampshire by Mary Sumner in 1876. Only two out of nearly sixty mothers have been identified: Mrs Dubber (two from right, seated) holding Bob and Mrs Langridge (three from the right) holding Roy. Hooke Hall belonged to the Streatfeilds but was leased to Sir Frederick and Lady Parry.

Left: The Scout movement was started by the hero of Mafeking, Robert Baden-Powell, when he took a dozen boys for an experimental camp on Brownsea Island in 1907. In Uckfield the first troop was 1st Ridgewood (formed in 1909). In 1927 a patrol led by Lew Gale won the County Camping Competition. Standing (left to right): Ian Wilkie, Bill Henderson, Miss Wilson (S.M.) and Bill Packham. Seated: Bill Fox, Lew Gale and Peter Henderson.

Below: Robert Baden-Powell's sister, Agnes, was the founder of the Girl Guide movement in 1910. The 2nd Uckfield Guide Company was formed in 1919. For five years (1925-1930) Miss Nessie Clarke was Captain and the company normally met in St Saviour's Hall (but is seen here in the garden at Ulverstone House in 1927). Miss Clarke's use of the whistle to summon the girls had to be discontinued as it was also the signal for the Fire Brigade.

The Boys' Brigade predated the Scout Movement by some 24 years, being launched by William Smith at the Free College Church Mission in Glasgow in 1883. It was to Sir William that Baden-Powell turned for advice when Scouting began. In Uckfield the Boys' Brigade were the later starters, in November, 1937. The Company numbered 14 at their first inspection by Mr Jeff Knight. Front row (4th from left): Leslie Hazelden, Ted Burtenshaw, Robert Crowhurst, Robert Browning, Bert Fry. Back row (visible): Maurice Wren, J. Waters, Eric Row, Henry Turner and H. Smith.

Within a year of its foundation that Uckfield Company had twenty boys under the leadership of Jeff Knight. Back row, left to right: D. Carter, D. Bates, E. Dadswell, P. Chatfield, C. Fry. Standing (middle row): W. Bond, L. Hazelden, E. Burtenshaw, L. Frost, D. Spreadbury, R. Crowhurst, G. Deadman, H. Turner, E. Rowe, E. Kenward. Seated: M. Wren, C. Walton, Rev. J. Beeby (Chaplain), J.H. Knight, H.W. Joslin (President), R.C. Brown, S. Crowhurst. Seated on ground: R. Browning, G. Frost, I. Crowhurst, R. Langridge, B. Fry.

Without the threat of 'Payment by Results' hanging over them, elementary schools (as they were known until 1944) could afford to be more ambitious in their curricula, even though Reading, Writing and Arithmetic (the three Rs) continued to hold pride of place. There was more encouragement, too (influenced by Montessori, Pestalozzi, Froebel and other educational reformers) for teachers to involve children in activities that were not strictly academic. One can scarcely doubt the enjoyment of these children (photographed in front of Buxted Park House) in the performance of *Once upon a time*.

St Michael's School was a breakaway from Rose Hill at Tunbridge Wells soon after the First World War. Under the headship of the euphoniously named Harold Hubert Hibbert Hockey (known as Mr Bean) the school moved into the premises vacated by the Agricultural College. In Fathers v Sons matches two conventions were normally observed: Fathers batted with cut-down bats; sons were given the opportunity to bowl at (but not necessarily to dismiss) their own fathers. In 1940 the school moved to Barnstaple where it is still going strong.

Uckfield Grammar School experienced the vicissitudes common to many such schools in small towns in the nineteenth century. At one stage it was forced to close due to defective sanitary arrangements, but money from the sale of Rocks Farm enabled dormitories to be built over a new gymnasium and from 1885, when the school reopened under a vigorous new headmaster, Hugh Isbister Smith, it gained and kept a high reputation both for its academic achievements and for its sporting prowess. One just hopes that the masters competing in the school cross-country race (in 1928) were doing so voluntarily.

The syllabus for a school in the early twentieth century was a remarkably wide one including drawing, carpentry, military drill, singing, gymnastics and swimming in the river while shorthand tuition was available. But there were economic pressures on small schools and in spite of an injection of vitality by a new young head, Dr McGregor Williams, in 1928, the school closed two years later. The memorial to Old Boys who fell in the First World War was transferred to Holy Cross Church.

Near the southern end of the High Street stood a wheelwright's shop, founded by Henry and Napkin Brooker and later taken on by Henry's son, James Saxby Brooker. The site eventually became the Uckfield Bus Terminus used by Southdown, East Surrey and Autocar Services, all of whose buses ran on solid tyres. Opposite stands the garage of French and Thurlow, Automobile Engineers. On the left of the picture notice the Cardale Memorial (see p.88).

When the war ended, scores of ex-Army vehicles (mostly solid-tyred) were released for sale to the general public. Landlords of public houses were frequent purchasers since they could provide garaging – and customers. On 1 June 1921, it was Derby Day and about two dozen patrons of the Alma Arms prepared to travel 50 miles, there and back, to Epsom in acute discomfort to enjoy a day out.

The Uckfield Motor Cycle and Car Club was founded in 1920 by a group of young enthusiasts which included Guy Bridger, Bill Clark, Stanley Durrant, Ron Hodge, Stanley French, Bill Rice, Tom Taylor, Guy Tyhurst and Henry Bingham Towner. The club promoted interclub trials, this picture showing a group of members and visitors assembled at Buxted Station (1926).

There was disagreement locally over whether Sainsbury's and Mence Smith were taking it in turns to wreck the level crossing gates, or whether it was regarded as a contest with points awarded in proportion to damage done. On this occasion (12 August 1933) Sainsbury's scored heavily when the brakes of their grocery van failed as it came down the High Street, not only wrecking the gates and the van, but doing considerable damage to the 5.20am goods train coming through from Lewes. Amazingly no one was hurt.

Friendly Societies originated in the late eighteenth century. Their aim was to help and encourage poor working men to 'put a bit by' for times when they were sick or unemployed or too old to work. Two of the most famous were the Independent Order of Oddfellows and the Ancient Order of Foresters. The Foresters' Hall in Harcourt Road (the property of the local Court of Foresters) was built in 1904. With a seating capacity of 400 it could be hired out for concerts and it did, in fact, serve as Uckfield's first cinema. This postcard was written by the caretaker's son, S.J. Crowhurst.

The Picture House was built in 1916, at a time when silent films were becoming increasingly popular but the application of the owner, Miss Measures, to operate a cinema was refused by the magistrates, one of whom already had a licence to show films at the Foresters' Hall. Finally, in 1920, the licence was granted and by 1930 the 'talkies' had reached Uckfield.

Richard James Streatfeild continued to be a major employer of labour both at The Rocks mansion and on his 2,000 acre estate. Among the projects he undertook was the rebuilding of the footbridge over the road to Isfield (1923). Here at its successful conclusion are seen: George Weaver (carpenter), George Warnett, James Dubber (painter), -?-, Arch Durrant and Ernest Langridge (bricklayer).

Uplands was the home of the Scarlett family. Their main property was at Gigha in Argyllshire but they also had a big house on the outskirts of Uckfield. Mary Scarlett, daughter of John Williams Scarlett, married Richard James Streatfeild in 1865. When their daughter, Annette, died in 1937, the Streatfeild estates passed to Mary's great-nephew, James Scarlett, who took the additional name of Streatfeild. Whist became increasingly popular in the late nineteenth and early twentieth century, being less intellectually taxing than bridge.

The Uckfield Carnival Society traces its origins back to 1827 when it was first organised on a Wednesday afternoon (the traditional early closing day). It appears to have merged in due course with the more exuberant Bonfire Society. Both organisations gave full scope to people's love of dressing up. The ingenious costumes on display here, incorporating letters, postcards, parcels and even a huge inkwell, were made and worn by the staff of Ganders.

The Bonfire Society received a setback when blazing tar barrels (see p.78) were no longer permitted to be rolled down the High Street. But the processions continued (with 'No Popery' banners much in evidence) and indeed were encouraged by the gentry and the clergy. Since the First World War the Carnival Society has continued to sustain the festival spirit while focusing on early September rather than 5 November.

This vehicle predated Norman Tebbitt's exhortation to 'get on your bike' by at least sixty years and in this case Fred Thorpe was in search of business rather than work. Not content with setting up a Drapers' and Outfitters' business in Framfield Road he set off on motor-cycle and sidecar to supply the clothing needs of the neighbouring villages.

Dr Sweet joined Drs Lucas and Langdale in the Uckfield practice, c. 1900 and established his surgery at his own home, The Meads, in Grange Road. A greatly respected GP, Dr Sweet was equally renowned as a motorist, his motor cars lovingly cared for by William Dutson, shown here standing beside the Austro Daimler limousine (c. 1925).

The story of Uckfield between the First and Second World Wars (as of many essentially rural communities) is of a hesitant advance into the modern world with many a backward glance at the kind of life that was disappearing forever. Here, though, is a scene that can scarcely have changed in centuries, Mr Cornford ploughing at Harlands Farm.

Another scene that could well have come from earlier centuries, but was actually photographed in the mid 1930s, Mr West's hoop-makers at work. His business, near the east end of Framfield Road, advertised itself as that of coal, coke, wood and hoop merchant, carrier and contractor. Mr West is in the centre, wearing a hat.

Plashett Park is first recorded in 1285. For hundreds of years it belonged to the Gage family and then, in 1902, it passed to the Christie family. The Park had long been renowned for the quality of its oak trees, the main timber itself being used for the construction of timber-framed buildings, the smaller branches in the production of charcoal and the bark carefully stripped off and sold to a nearby tannery.

After the First World War Thomas Veness managed the sawmill for the Christies. Young Tom (seen here at the wheel) eventually took over from his father and, although continuing the business mostly in the traditional fashion, did introduce some mechanisation. In fact the vehicle he is seen driving was an Austin twin-axle lorry, designed for ease of loading. They were first manufactured in 1915 and many of them were sent out to Russia which was experiencing desperate transport problems on the Eastern Front.

Luther White, leader of the Fire Brigade, tax assessor and blacksmith, handed over the smithy to John Hills, *c.* 1870 and he in turn to Alfred Charles Cole in 1906. The group here are (left to right): James Napthali Funnell, Herbert Crowhurst (son of Thomas, the Framfield vet), Alfred Cole, George Discombe and John Hills (the son). Mr Cole lived at Rock Cottage, next to the forge.

Throughout the First World War the smithy worked closely with the army farriers (see p.112) and even after the war there were always plenty of horses waiting to be shod in addition to the blacksmith's many other tasks. George Discombe took over from Alfred Cole in around 1935 but did not, apparently, live at Rock Cottage. Fred Miles was the last blacksmith to work the forge which finally closed in 1962. Unlike many others it never turned itself into a garage.

Dr Charles Leeson Prince (see p.60) recorded severe flooding of the river on six occasions between 1843 and 1860. 'The whole of the brook land between Uckfield and Buxted bridges presented one sheet of water', he recorded in November 1844. At least eight major floodings have been recorded in the twentieth century. This photograph was taken before 1922 when Ebenezer Warburton (who succeeded Edwin Kenward) replaced the middle section of the Roller Mill with a four-storey building.

Almost the last housing development to be completed before the outbreak of World War Two was the building of Keld Close and Keld Avenue. The whole undertaking was planned by Stanley Durrant and carried out after his father's death in 1937. A scene of almost incredible (if momentarily frozen) energy is shown here with bricklayers, carpenters, plasterers and painters all busily employed.

R.J. STREATFEILD ESQ.

The Streatfeilds were the leading family in Uckfield for a century, but their active participation was confined to the lifetime of Richard James (1844-1931). As a young man he had served in the Dragoon Guards and during the First World War he raised the Uckfield Volunteer Training Corps. He first became a JP in 1866, an office he held for 65 years. From 1895 to 1920 he was chairman of Uckfield Urban District Council and he served on, and chaired, a wide range of bodies extending throughout East Sussex. In Uckfield he is best remembered as a landowner considerate to his tenants and as a benefactor, giving the land for the Victoria Pleasure Ground, for the Uckfield Institute, for the Public Hall and for the Cottage Hospital. He was a Governor of the Grammar School for sixty years and vigorously opposed its closure. He also offered the Cricket Club and the Boy Scouts facilities at The Rocks, while his only daughter, Annette, ran the Wolf Cubs for many years.

R.J. Streatfeild died on 31 July 1931. His coffin was carried on an estate wagon from The Rocks to Holy Cross Church and when Annette died only six years later Mr W.A. Clark (of the estate agents St John Smith) persuaded a consortium of four local businessmen to purchase the whole estate (2,115 acres). The estate was then divided up for resale by auction in November, 1938. As a result, many townspeople and tenant farmers were enabled to buy their own properties. At a stroke Uckfield gained more than a hundred new freeholders, but by then the menace of Hitler was dwarfing people's everyday concerns.